W9-BJV-056

Roger Quilter
55 Songs

High Voice

Edited by Richard Walters

This publication is not for sale in the
EU or other European countries.

ISBN 0-634-06008-2

HAL•LEONARD®
CORPORATION
7777 W. BLUEMOUND RD. P.O. BOX 13819 MILWAUKEE, WI 53213

Visit Hal Leonard Online at
www.halleonard.com

Contents
by Opus Number

Because "Prelude" and "Interlude" from *To Julia* are piano only, they are not tallied in the "55 Songs" of the title of this volume.

Contents
Alphabetically by Song Title

Poet Index

Roger Quilter (born 1 November 1877, died 21 September 1953) was a breed of composer that has rarely existed after the first decades of the twentieth century: he was overwhelmingly concerned with the art song. His preoccupation with the genre spanned more than fifty years, from his youth until near his death, more than fifty years later, resulting in roughly 140 songs in total.

Quilter was born into a wealthy family in Sussex, England. His father, William Cuthbert Quilter, was a prominent, very successful businessman, art collector and member of Parliament, and was knighted Sir Quilter by Queen Victoria in 1897. There were seven children in the Quilter home who survived past infancy, two girls and five boys. Roger was fifth oldest. This tall, lanky, sensitive, artistic boy was miserable in the traditional, sports-minded population of males at Eton College. He went abroad to study composition with Ivann Knorr in Frankfurt at the Hoch Conservatory. Fellow students there, at different times, included Percy Grainger, Balfour Gardiner, Norman O'Neill and Cyril Scott. Grainger, particularly, became a lifelong close friend of Quilter's.

A public career began for Quilter with the 1901 London premiere of *Songs of the Sea*, not surprisingly the composer's choice for the designation of Opus 1. Gervase Elwes, a celebrated tenor, became interested in Quilter songs. For him the composer wrote the song cycle *To Julia*, which Elwes premiered in 1905. The same singer gave the first performance of the *Seven Elizabethan Lyrics* in 1908. Quilter's music soon gained favor, and his songs were regularly performed, particularly in London. A good pianist, the composer often served as accompanist in recital. Quilter's wide social circles included just about any musician of note who worked in London in the first decades of the twentieth century.

Due to inheritance, Quilter never had to seek employment, leaving his time and mind free for composing, though his life was not always a happy one. His wealth was limited, and in later years he was often in debt. He was plagued by chronic poor health throughout his life, which prevented military service during World War I. Quilter was a well-mannered, sophisticated gentleman, with the polish of his well-to-do social class, but with a constantly observable nervousness. He suffered unstable periods, with pronounced mental illness in the years leading to his death. A homosexual, he never married, though he formed a few close attachments and had devoted friends and supporters.

The composer's chamber instrumental and orchestral output was limited; most was light in nature. Most were arrangements of music composed for other genres. Quilter also composed piano pieces, small choral works, two ballets, and incidental theatre music, notably for *Where the Rainbow Ends*, a children's fairy play with music first produced in 1911, with annual Christmastime revivals in London until 1959. (Noel Coward was in the original cast.) The composer collaborated on the light opera *Julia*, which premiered in 1936 at the Royal Opera House in London, but to not much success.

Quilter valued graceful elegance and a love of words, both qualities that are evident in his songs and his idiomatic phrasing for the voice. The imagery in his songs constantly reflects his boyhood countryside of southern England. He was uninterested in the more extreme and progressive artistic trends of the twentieth century. In general, though there are exceptions, he showed a rather refined literary taste in poetry chosen for his songs, with an inherent nationalist British identification. Quilter's fluid and distinctive musical style, though occasionally dramatic, is most often infused with a natural, creamy English charm, though he did not compose quickly, and labored over every detail. Most agree that his best work was created rather young in his life, before his mid-forties.

Today Quilter would be considered a minor historical figure in British music overall. Regarding art song, however, very few composers working in English have matched his achievement of a living body of beloved, relevant, literate repertoire.

RW

To my mother

THE SEA-BIRD

from Three Songs of the Sea, Op. 1

original key: E minor

Words and Music by
Roger Quilter
Op. 1, No. 1

Sun - sets gold - en floor.

mf

I

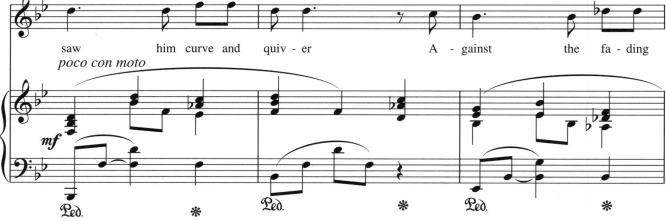

poco con moto

saw him curve and quiv - er A - gainst the fa - ding

mf

poco con moto

poco cresc.

sky, And heard the sad waves shiv - er

poco cresc.

cresc.

f

Un - der his death like cry.

cresc.

f

To my mother

MOONLIGHT

from Three Songs of the Sea, Op. 1

original key: D Major

Words and Music by
Roger Quilter
Op. 1, No. 2

Moderato (♩ = 88)

Un - der the sil - ver moon - light Flut - ter the great white wings. Wood dry by soft night breez - es Ten - der with whis - per'd

Whis - per, O soft night breez - es. Mur - mur your ten - der

tune, _____ Car - ry the white wings

on - ward Un - der the sil - ver moon.

To my mother

BY THE SEA

from Three Songs of the Sea, Op. 1

original key: D minor

Words and Music by
Roger Quilter
Op. 1, No. 3

Poco allegro con moto (♩. = 72)

mf

risoluto

mf

I stood to-day by the shim-m'ring

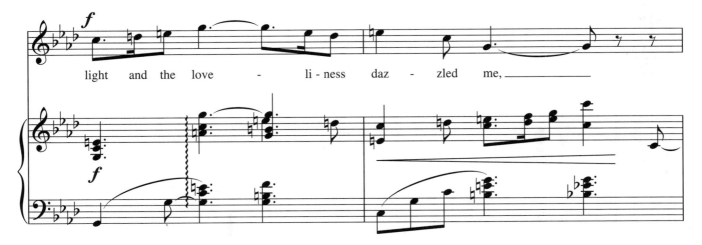

sea; ___ Nev-er was wind ___ so mild and free; ___ The

f

light and the love-li-ness daz-zled me, ___

f

daz - led me. The

waves did fro - lic _____ and curl and roll; _____ They sigh'd and sang _____ to my

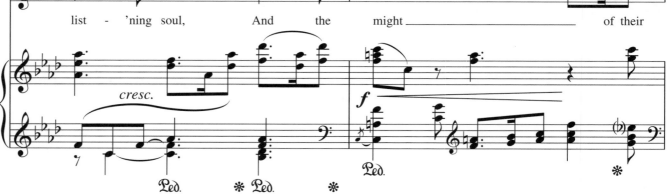

list - 'ning soul, And the might _____ of their

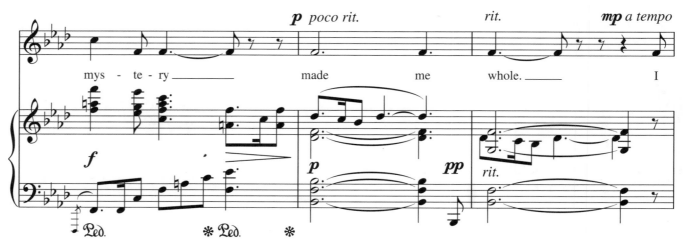

mys - te - ry _____ made me whole. _____ I

poco cresc.

stood to-day by the shim-m'ring sea; _____ Nev - er was

mp *a tempo*

poco cresc.

cresc.

wind _____ so mild _____ and free; _____ The

cresc.

light and the love - li-ness daz-zled me, _____ daz - zled

f

f

f

f

me.

vigoroso

ff

sff *sff*

Ped. * Ped.

COME BACK!
from Two Songs (1903)
original key

Words and Music by
Roger Quilter

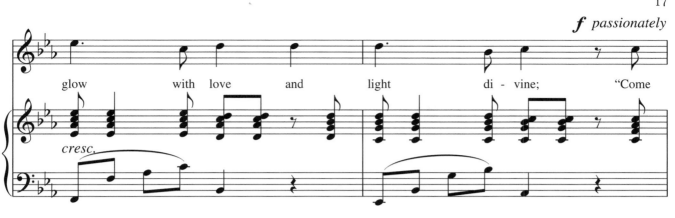

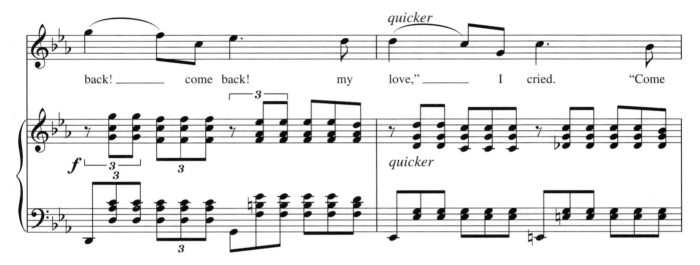

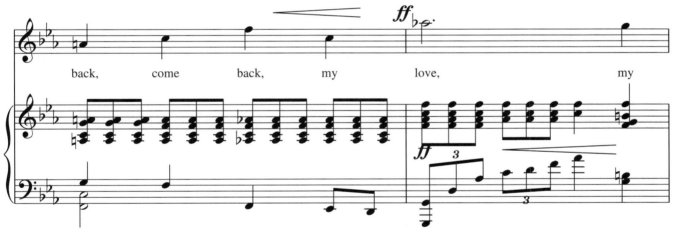

A SECRET

from Two Songs (1903)

original key: E-flat Major

Words and Music by
Roger Quilter

My heart, my heart No one may see, It is lock'd a-

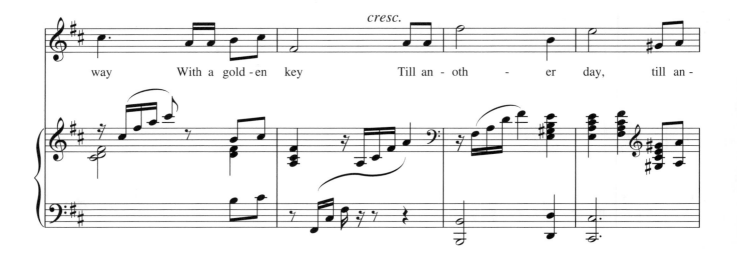

way With a gold-en key Till an-oth-er day, till an-

oth-er day: _____ When my love shall come, As a

bird to its mate, With the gold-en key, And un-lock the gate. __ And the

world shall see! My heart, my heart No one may

see, It is lock'd a-way With a gold-en key Till an-oth - er, an-

oth - er day! _____

To Gervase Elwes

LOVE'S PHILOSOPHY

from Three Songs, Op. 3

original key

Words by
Percy B. Shelley

Music by
Roger Quilter
Op. 3, No. 1

sweet e - mo - tion. No - thing in the world is

sin - gle; All things, by a law di - vine, In one an -

o - ther's be - ing min - gle,— Why not I _____ with

thine, not I, _____ with thine?

See, the

moun - tains kiss high Heav'n, _____ And the

waves ____ clasp one an - o - ther; No sis - ter flower would be for -

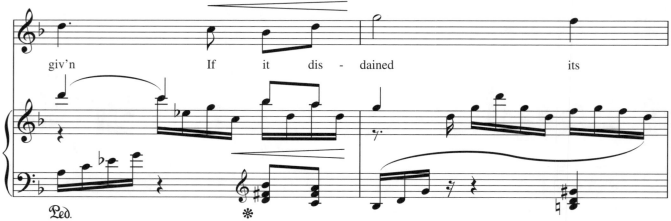

giv'n   If   it   dis - dained   its

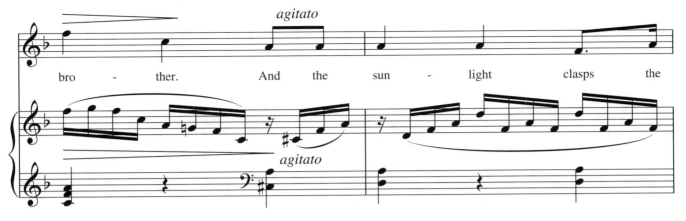

agitato

bro - ther. And the sun - light clasps the

earth, And the moon - beams kiss the

cresc.

sea, _____ What are all these kiss - ings

worth, _____ If

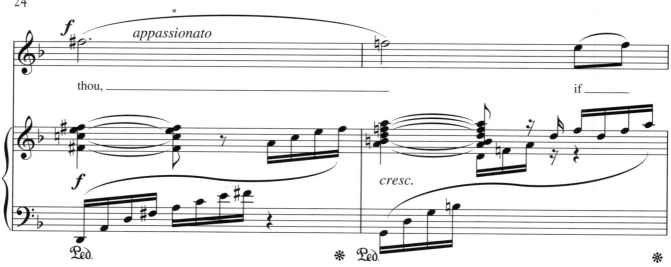

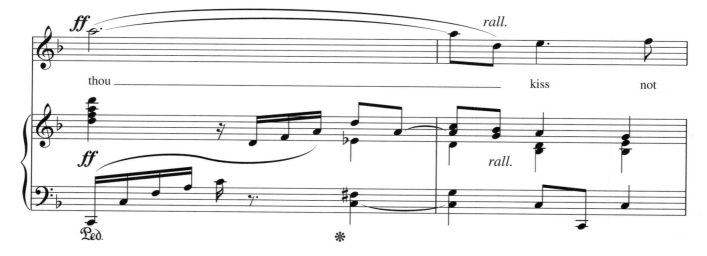

To Mrs. E.P. Balmain

NOW SLEEPS THE CRIMSON PETAL

from Three Songs, Op. 3

original key: E-flat Major

Words by
Alfred Tennyson

Music by
Roger Quilter
Op. 3, No. 2

Moderato quasi andantino (♩ = 60) tempo rubato

Now sleeps the crim-son pe-tal, not the white; _____

Nor waves the cy-press in the pa-lace walk; _____

Nor winks the gold fin in the porph'-ry font: The

fire - fly wa - kens: wa - ken thou with

me. con passione f

Now folds the li - ly all her sweet - ness up,

To Miss Ada Crossley

JUNE

original key: D Major

Words by
Nora Hopper

Music by
Roger Quilter
1905

In moderate time

Dark red ro - ses in a hon - eyed wind swing - ing,

Silk - soft hol - ly - hock, co - loured like the moon;

Larks high o-ver-head lost in light, and sing - ing;

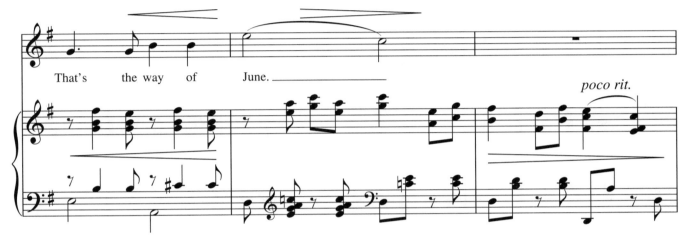

That's the way of June.

poco rit.

mp a tempo

Dark red ro - ses in the warm wind fall - ing,

a tempo

a little slower

Vel - vet leaf by vel - vet leaf, all the breath - less noon;

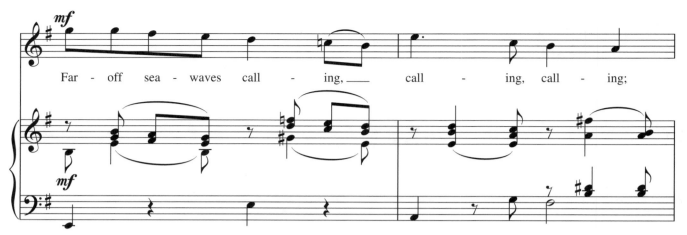

Far - off sea - waves call - ing, _____ call - ing, call - ing;

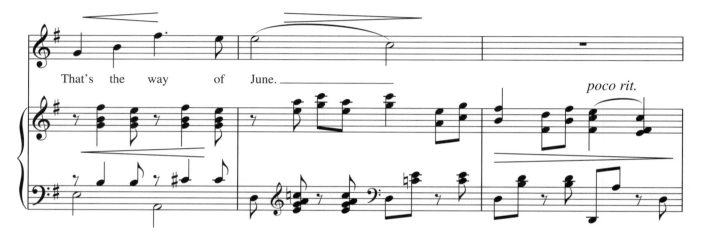

That's the way of June. _____

poco rit.

pp a tempo
opt.

Sweet as scar - let straw - ber - ry un - der wet leaves hid - den,

pp a tempo

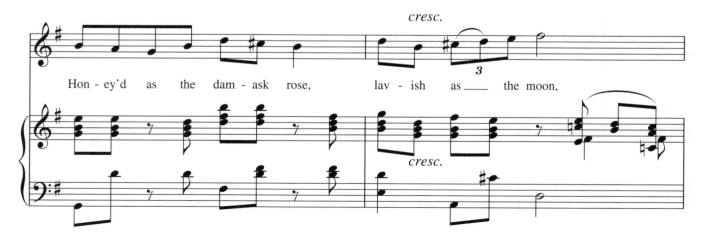

cresc.

Hon - ey'd as the dam - ask rose, lav - ish as ___ the moon,

cresc.

Shed - ding love - ly light on things for - got - ten, hope for -

bid - den, That's _____ the way of

June, the way, _____ the way _____ of

June. _____

To my sister, Norah

A GOOD CHILD

from Four Child Songs, Op. 5

original key

Words by
Robert Louis Stevenson

Music by
Roger Quilter
Op. 5, No. 1

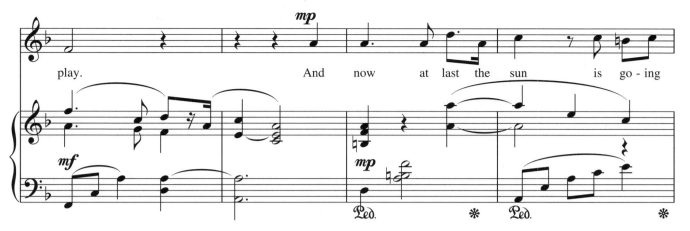

play. And now at last the sun is go-ing

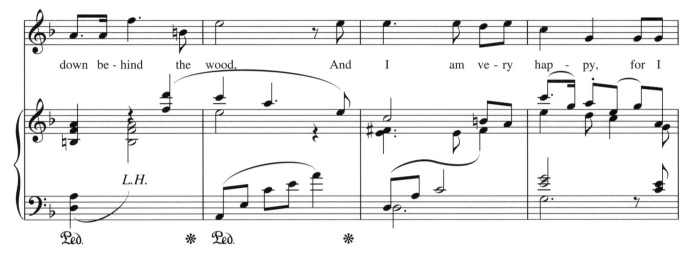

down be-hind the wood, And I am ve-ry hap-py, for I

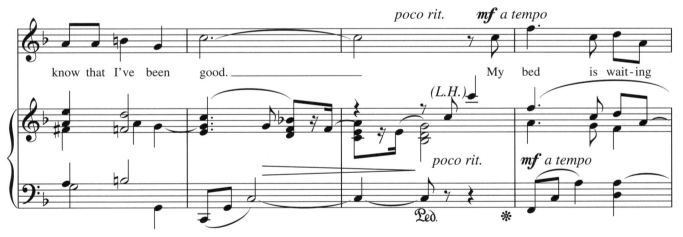

poco rit. **mf** *a tempo*

know that I've been good. My bed is wait-ing

cool and fresh, with lin-en smooth and fair, And

I must off to sleep a-gain, and not for-get my prayer, and

poco rit. **p**

not for-get my prayer. I know that, till to-

poco rit. **mp** *a tempo* **p**

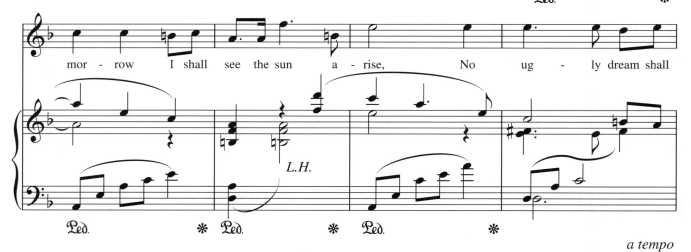

mor - row I shall see the sun a - rise, No ug - ly dream shall

L.H.

poco rit. *a tempo* *a tempo* *poco rit.* **mf**

fright my mind, no ug - ly sight my eyes, But

poco rit. *a tempo* *poco rit.*

L.H.

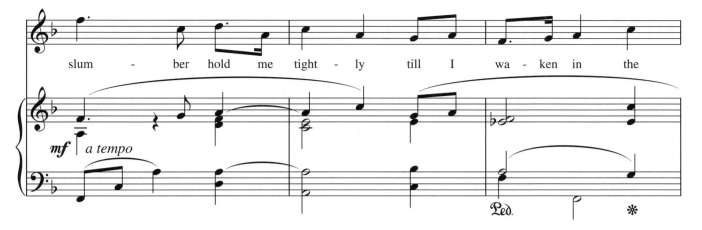

slum - ber hold me tight - ly till I wa - ken in the

dawn, And hear the thrush - es sing - ing, and hear the thrush - es

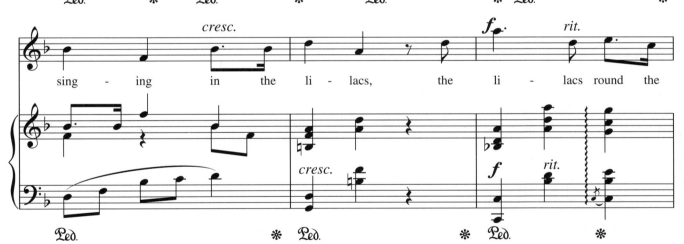

sing - ing in the li - lacs, the li - lacs round the

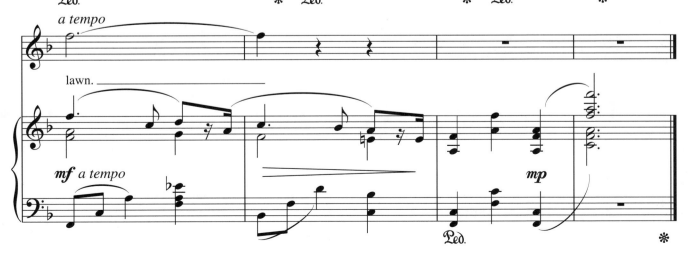

lawn.

To my sister, Norah

THE LAMPLIGHTER

from Four Child Songs, Op. 5

original key

Words by
Robert Louis Stevenson

Music by
Roger Quilter
Op. 5, No. 2

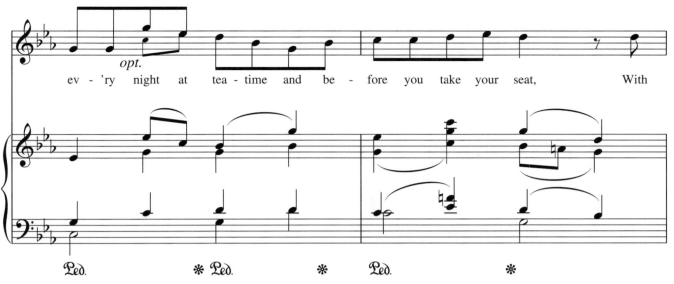

ev -'ry night at tea - time and be - fore you take your seat, With

lan - tern and with lad - der he comes post - ing up the street, comes

poco rit.   *a tempo*

post - ing up the street. ___ Now

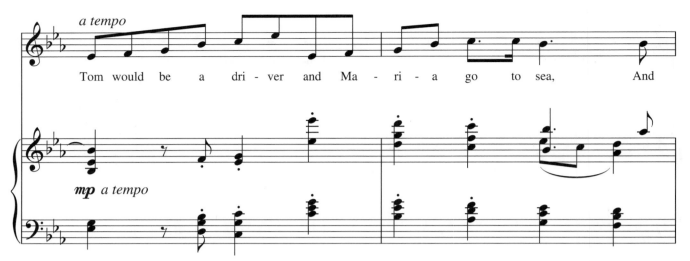

Tom would be a dri - ver and Ma - ri - a go to sea, And

my pa - pa's a ban - ker and as rich as he can be; But

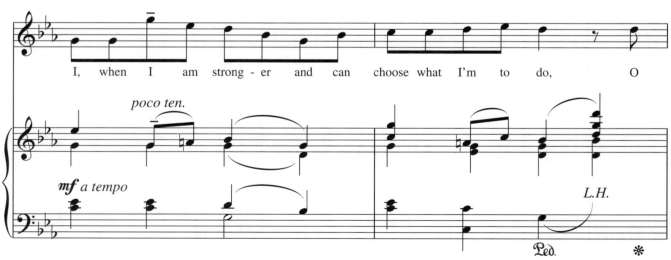

I, when I am strong - er and can choose what I'm to do, O

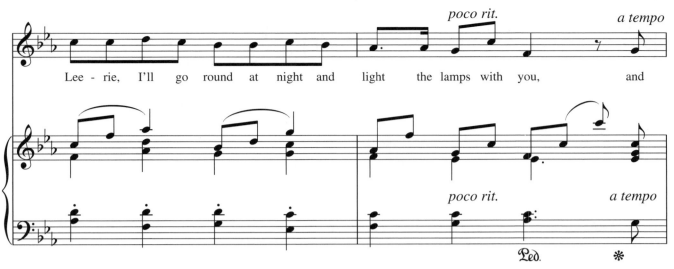

Lee - rie, I'll go round at night and light the lamps with you, and

light the lamps with you! ____ For

we are ve - ry luck - y, with a lamp be - fore the door, And

To my sister, Norah

WHERE GO THE BOATS?

from Four Child Songs, op. 5

original key

Words by
Robert Louis Stevenson

Music by
Roger Quilter
Op. 5, No. 3

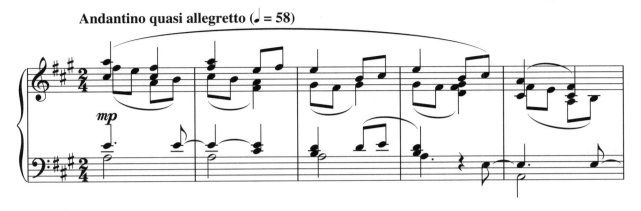

Dark brown is the riv-er, Gold-en is the sand. It

flows a-long for ev-er, With trees on ei-ther hand.

Green leaves a - float - ing, Cas - tles of the foam,

Boats of mine a - boat - ing— Where will all come home?

On goes the ri - ver And

out past the mill, A - way down the val - ley, A -

To Walter Creighton

COME AWAY, DEATH

from Three Shakespeare Songs, Op. 6 (First Set)

original key: C minor

Words by
William Shakespeare
from *Twelfth Night*

Music by
Roger Quilter
Op. 6, No. 1

Come a-way, come a-way, death, And in sad cy-press let me be laid; Fly a-way, fly a-way, breath; I am

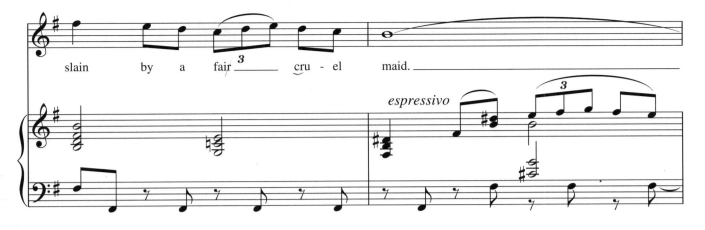

slain by a fair cru-el maid.

My shroud of white, stuck all with yew,

O pre-pare it; My part of death no

one so true Did share it.

46

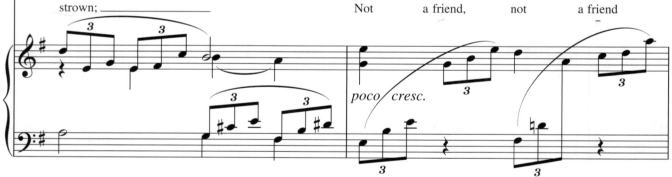

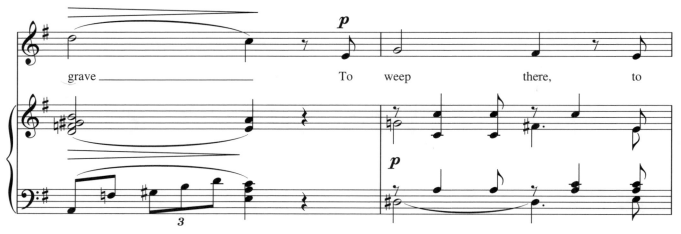

grave _____ To weep there, to

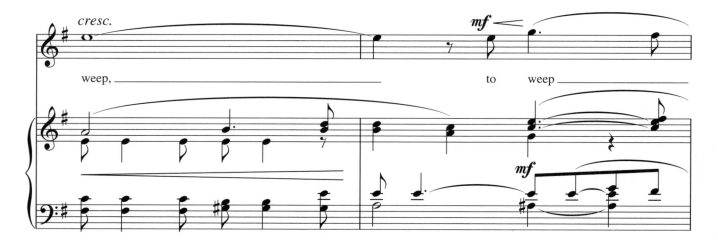

weep, _____ to weep _____

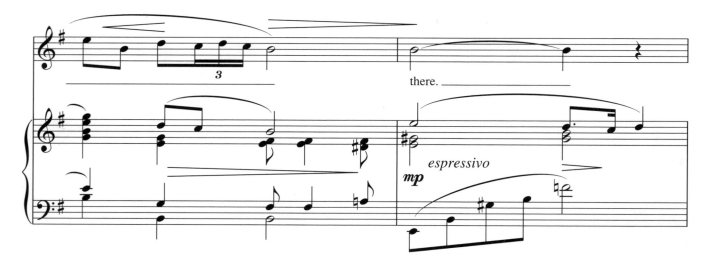

there. _____

To Walter Creighton

O MISTRESS MINE
from Three Shakespeare Songs, Op. 6 (First Set)
original key: E-flat Major

Words by
William Shakespeare
from *Twelfth Night*

Music by
Roger Quilter
Op. 6, No. 2

fur - ther, pret - ty sweet - ing; Jour - neys end in lov - ers'

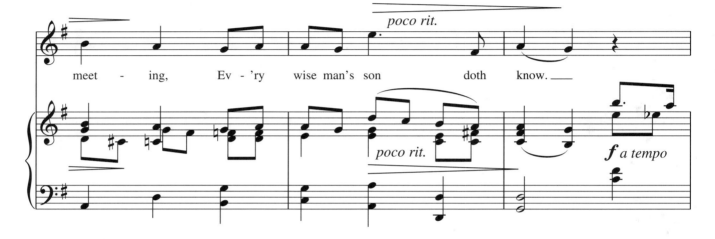

meet - ing, Ev - 'ry wise man's son doth know.

What is

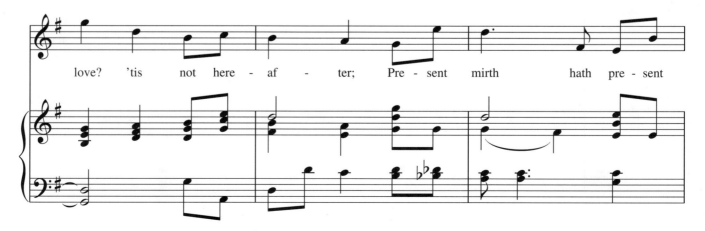

love? 'tis not here - af - ter; Pre - sent mirth hath pre - sent *cresc.*

laugh - ter; What's to come is still un - sure: In de -

cresc.

Ped. ✱

f

lay there lies no plen - ty; Then come kiss me, Sweet-and -

f

mf *poco rit.*

twen - ty, Youth's a stuff will not en - dure, not en - dure. ___

a tempo

mf *mp*

poco rit.

mp poco meno mosso

Mis - tress mine, where are you roam - ing?

rit.

poco meno mosso

p espressivo *pp*

Ped. ✱

To Walter Creighton

BLOW, BLOW, THOU WINTER WIND

from Three Shakespeare Songs, Op. 6 (First Set)

original key: C minor

Words by
William Shakespeare
from *As You Like It*

Music by
Roger Quilter
Op. 6, no. 3

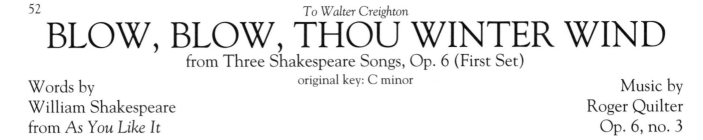

Non troppo allegro ma vigoroso e con moto (♩ = 76)

Blow, blow, thou win- ter wind, Thou art not so un-

kind As man's in- grat- i- tude;

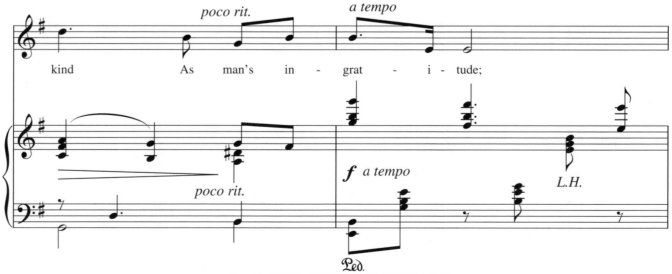

Thy tooth is not so keen, Be-

cause thou art not seen, Al - though thy breath be

rude, al - though thy breath be rude. _____

Poco più allegro (♩ = 88)

Heigh - ho! sing heigh - ho!

un - to the ___ green hol - ly; Most friend - ship is

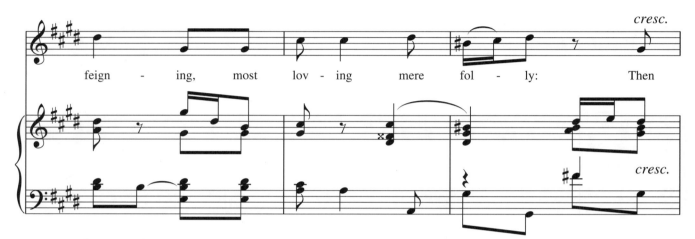

feign - ing, most lov - ing mere fol - ly: Then

heigh - ho! the hol - ly! This life this

life ___ is ___ most ___ jol - ly.

Tempo I

vigoroso

Freeze, freeze, thou bit - ter sky, That

dost not bite so nigh As be - ne - fits for -

poco rit.

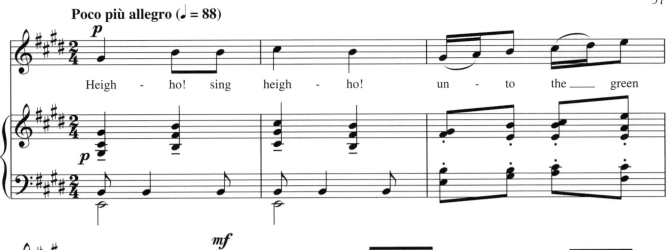

Poco più allegro (♩ = 88)

Heigh - ho! sing heigh - ho! un - to the ___ green

hol - ly: Most friend - ship is feign - ing, most

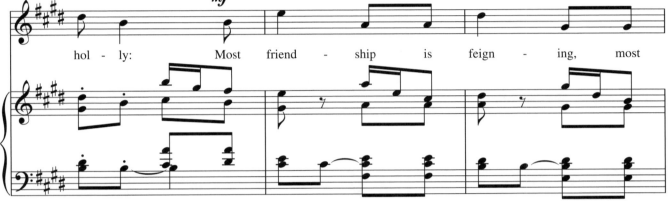

lov - ing mere fol - ly: Then heigh - ho! the

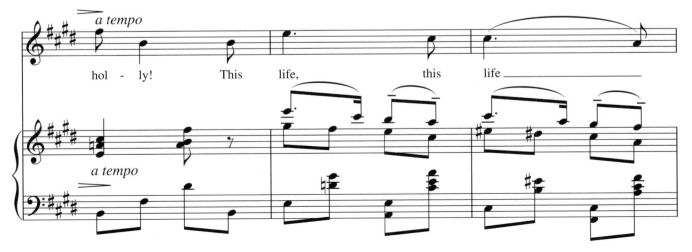

hol - ly! This life, this life ___

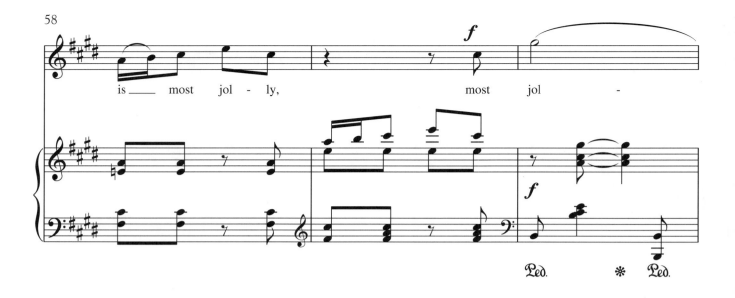

is ___ most jol - ly, most jol -

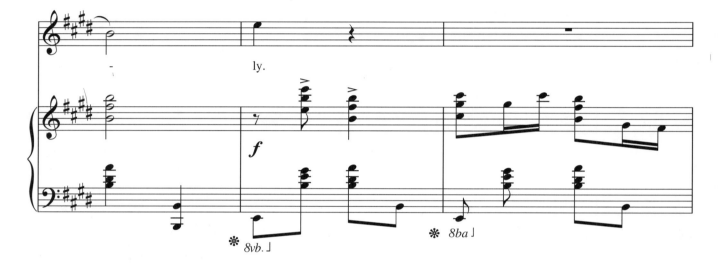

- ly.

molto vigoroso

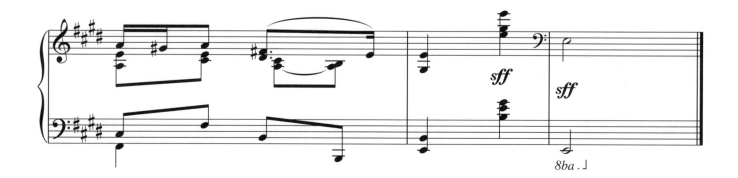

To Gervase Elwes

TO JULIA
Prelude
original key

Roger Quilter
Op. 8

Moderato tranquillo e con tenerezza (♩ = 69)

I. The Bracelet

from *To Julia*

original key

Words by
Robert Herrick

Music by
Roger Quilter
Op. 8, No. 1

Why I tie a-bout thy wrist, Ju - lia, this my ___

silk - en twist,   For ___ what

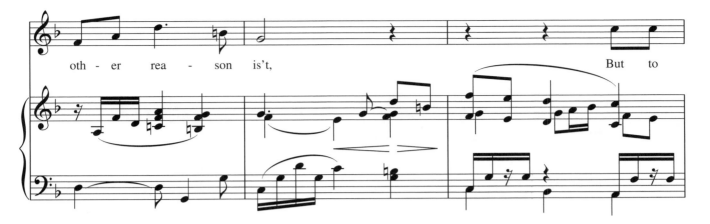

oth - er rea - son is't, But to

shew thee how in part Thou my pret - ty cap - tive

art? But thy bond - slave is my heart.

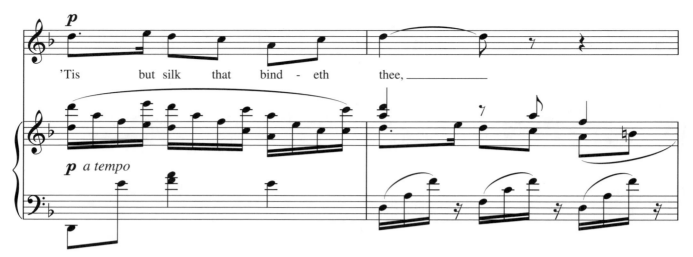

'Tis but silk that bind - eth thee, _____

Knap the thread and _____ thou art free _____

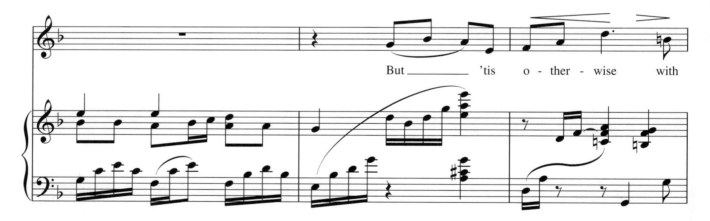

But _____ 'tis o - ther - wise with

me: I am bound, and fast bound

so .... That from thee I can - not go; _____ If I

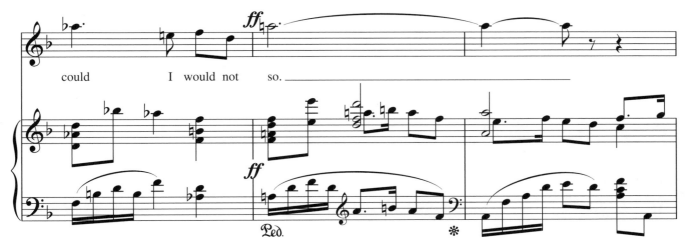

could .... I would not so. _____

II. The Maiden Blush

from *To Julia*

original key

Words by
Robert Herrick

Music by
Roger Quilter
Op. 8, No. 2

ru - bies late - ly pol - ish - ed:_____ So pur - est

di - a - per doth shine,_____ Stain'd by the beams_____ of clar - et wine: As

Ju - lia looks when she doth dress_____ Her ei - ther cheek, her ei - ther

cheek with bash - ful - ness._____

III. To Daisies

from *To Julia*

original key

Words by
Robert Herrick

Music by
Roger Quilter
Op. 8, No. 3

Shut not so soon, the dull-eyed night Has not as yet be-

gun   To make a seiz-ure on the light,

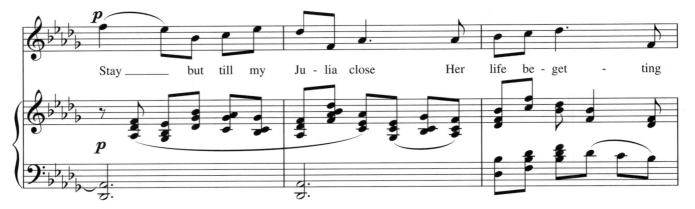

Stay _____ but till my Ju - lia close Her life be - get - ting

molto cresc.

eye; And let the whole world then dis - pose _____ It -

largamente

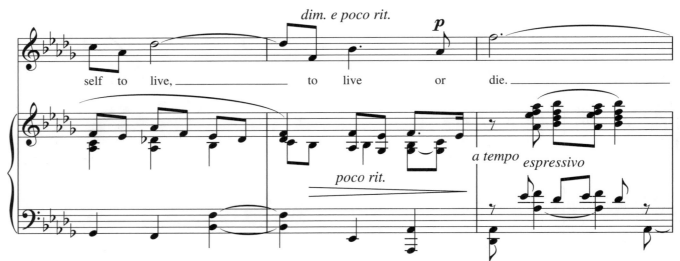

dim. e poco rit.

self to live, _____ to live or die. _____

poco rit.

a tempo espressivo

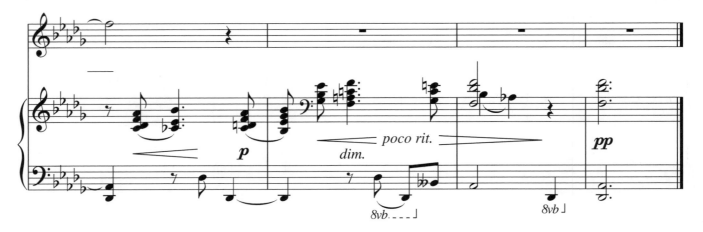

poco rit.

dim.

8vb. - - - ⌟   8vb ⌟

IV. The Night Piece

from *To Julia*

original key

Words by
Robert Herrick

Music by
Roger Quilter
Op. 8, No. 4

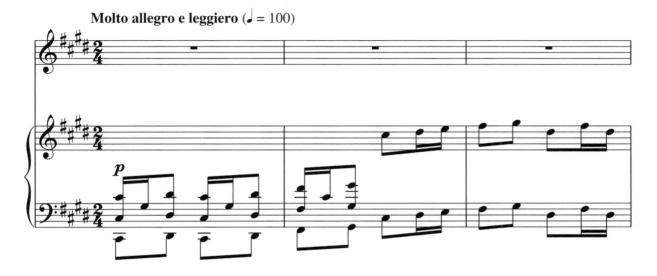

70

elves al - so, Whose lit - tle eyes glow Like the sparks of fire, the

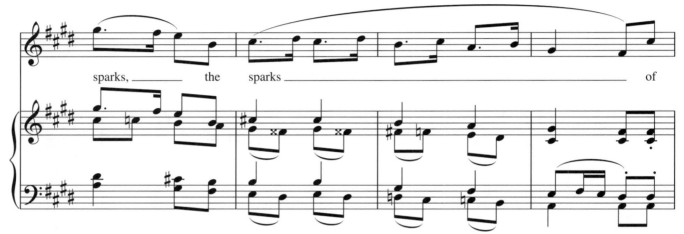

sparks, _____ the sparks _____ of

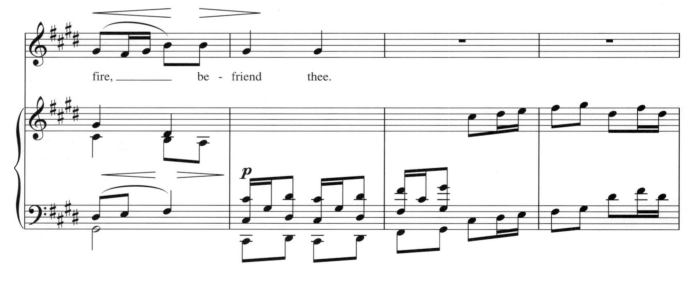

fire, _____ be - friend thee.

No will - o' - the - wisp mis - light thee, Nor

snake or slow - worm bite thee; But on, on thy way Not

cresc.

mak - ing a stay, Since ghost, ____ since ghost ____

mf

____ there's none ____ to af - fright thee.

mf *p* *L.H.*

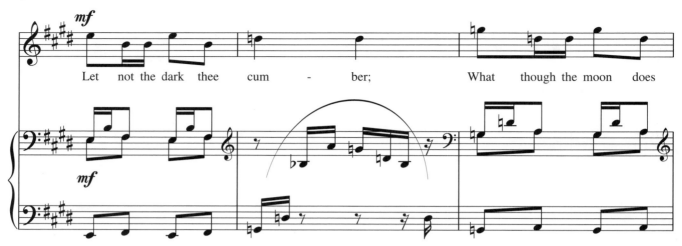

Let not the dark thee cum - ber; What though the moon does

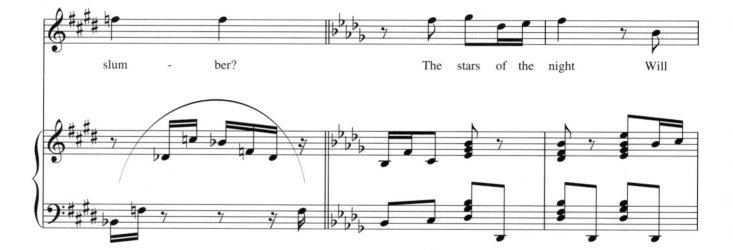

slum - ber? The stars of the night Will

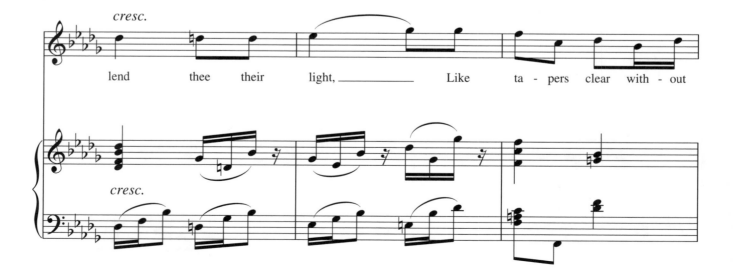

lend thee their light, _____ Like ta - pers clear with - out

num - ber.

Then,

cresc. poco rit.

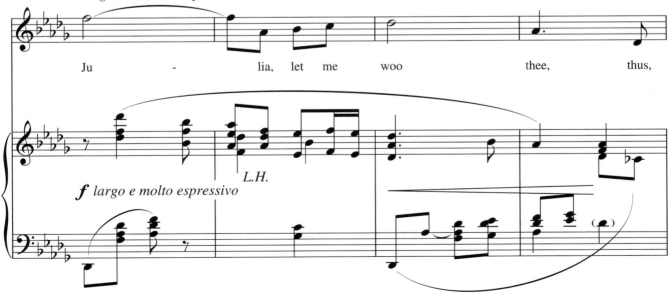

largo con molto espressione

Ju - lia, let me woo thee, thus,

L.H.

largo e molto espressivo

thus to come _____ un - to

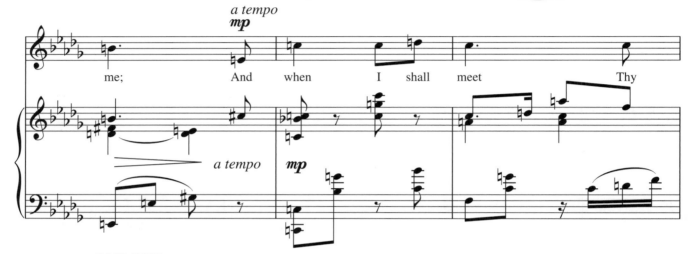

a tempo

me; And when I shall meet Thy

poco cresc. *cresc.*

sil - ver - y feet, My soul,

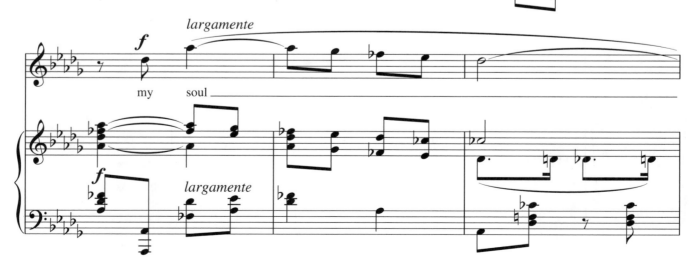

largamente

my soul _____

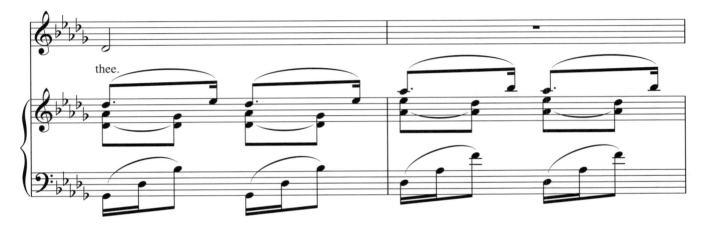

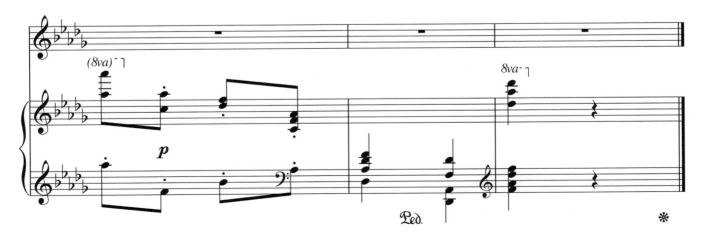

V. Julia's Hair

from *To Julia*

original key

Words by
Robert Herrick

Music by
Roger Quilter
Op. 8, No. 5

dew; Or glit-tered to my

sight, As when the beams Have their re-flect-ed

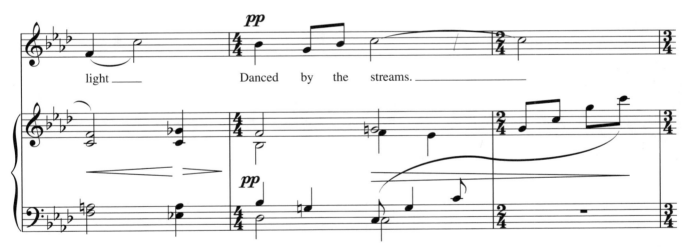

light _____ Danced by the streams. _____

Interlude
original key

Music by
Roger Quilter
Op. 8

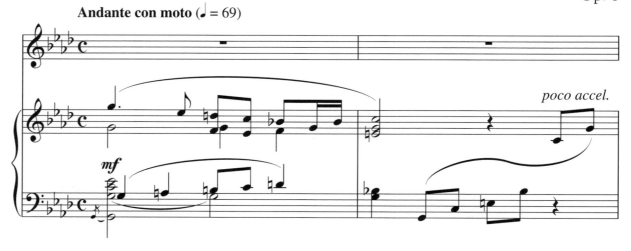

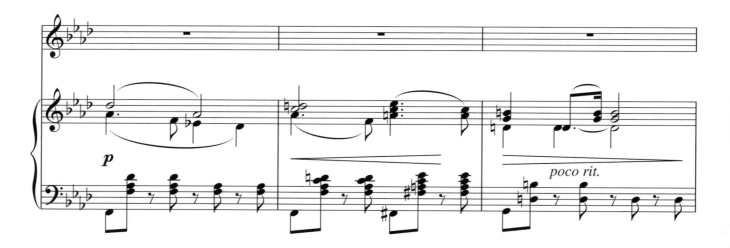

attacca, segue

VI. Cherry Ripe

from *To Julia*
original key

Words by
Robert Herrick

Music by
Roger Quilter
Op. 8, No. 6

Allegro con brio (♩ = 96)

"Cher - ry ripe, ripe," I cry,

"Full and fair ones, come and buy." If so be you ask me

where ____ They do grow, I an - swer: "There, Where my

Ju - lia's lips do smile;_____

cresc.

There's the land, or cher - ry - isle,

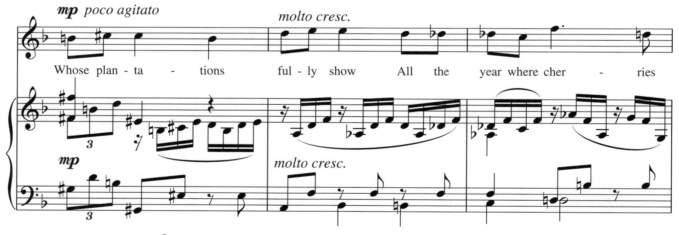

mp poco agitato   *molto cresc.*

Whose plan - ta - tions ful - ly show   All the year where cher - ries

mp   *molto cresc.*

grow."   "Cher - ry ripe, ripe," I cry,   "Full and

f

fair ones, come and buy, come _____ and buy."

"Where my Ju - lia's lips do smile; _____

There's the land, or cher - ry - isle, there's the land, or

cher - ry isle." _____

Tempo I

"Cher - ry ripe,

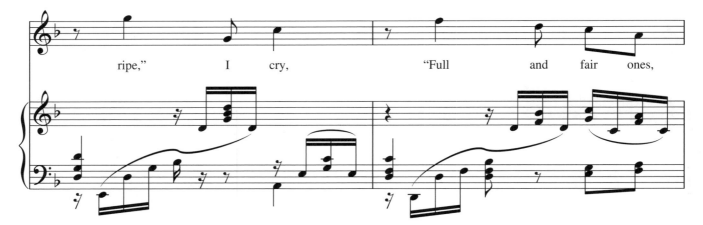

ripe," I cry, "Full and fair ones,

come and buy." If so be you ask me where _____ They do

grow, I an - swer: "There, Where my Ju - lia's lips do

smile; _____ There's the land, or cher - ry - isle,

Whose plan - ta - tions ful - ly show All the

year where cher - ries grow." "Cher - ry

ripe, ripe," I cry, "Full and

To the memory of my friend, Mrs. Cary-Elwes

THE FAITHLESS SHEPHERDESS

from Seven Elizabethan Songs, Op. 12

original key

Words Anonymous

Music by
Roger Quilter
Op. 12, No. 4

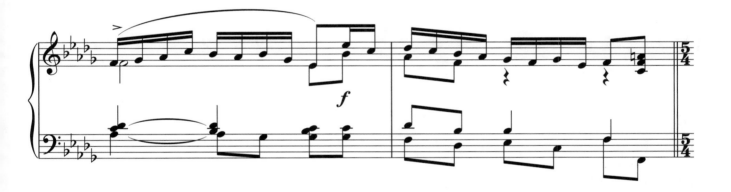

While that the sun ___ with his beams hot ___

Scorch-éd the fruits in vale and moun-tain, Phi-lon, the shep-herd, late for-got,

poco più tranquillo

Sit-ting be-side a cry-tal foun-tain, In sha-dow of a green oak

dolce

poco più tranquillo

tree, Up - on his pipe this song — play'd

ah

a tempo *f*

he: A - dieu, Love, a-dieu, Love, un-true — Love, Un-

a tempo
cresc.

f

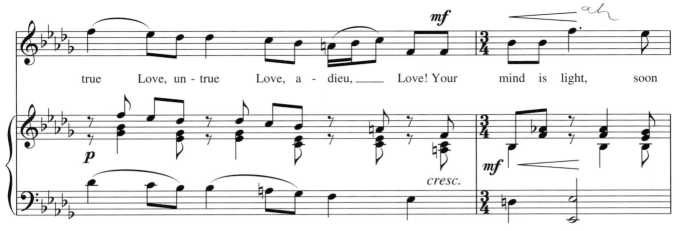

true Love, un-true Love, a-dieu,___ Love! Your mind is light, soon

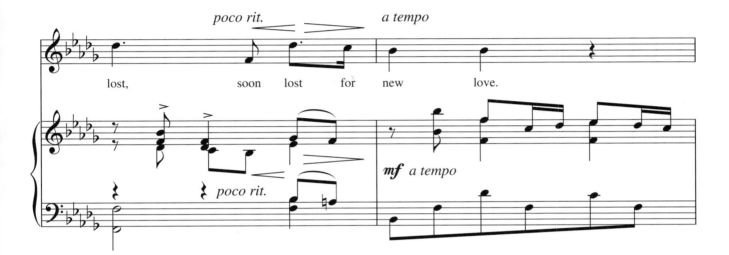

lost, soon lost for new love.

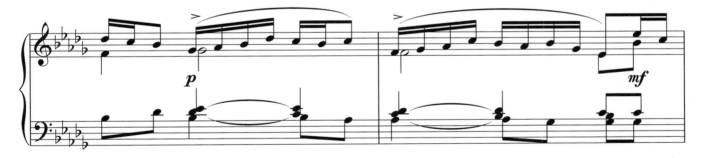

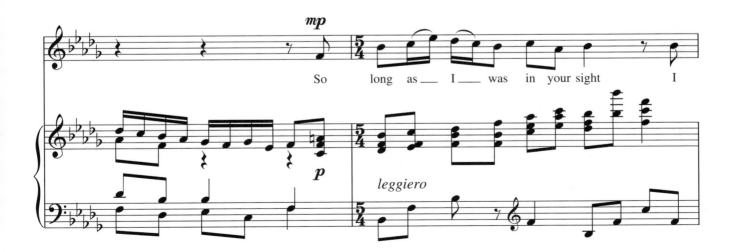

So long as _ I _ was in your sight I

espressivo

was your heart, your soul, your trea - sure; And ev - er-more you sobb'd and sigh'd

rit.

Burn - ing in flames be - yond all mea - sure: Three days en - dured your love to

cresc. *poco rit.*

me, And it was lost in o - ther

a tempo *f* *p*

three! A - dieu, Love, a - dieu, Love, un - true Love, Un -

cresc.

f

true Love, un-true Love, a - dieu,___ Love! Your mind is light, soon

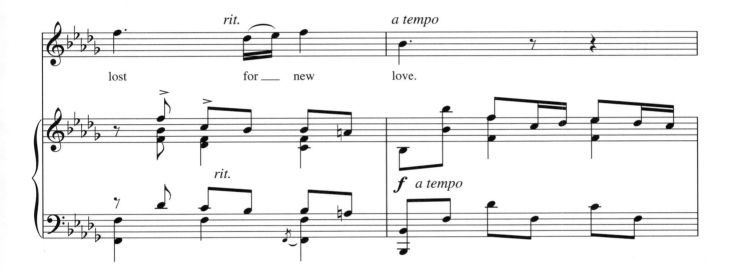

lost   for ___ new   love.

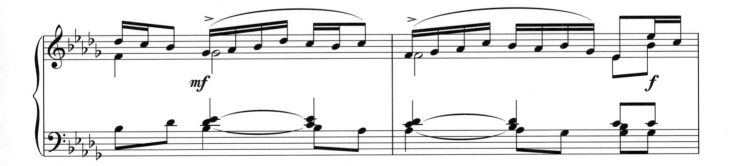

To the memory of my friend, Mrs. Cary-Elwes

WEEP YOU NO MORE

from Seven Elizabethan Songs, Op. 12

original key

Words Anonymous

Music by
Roger Quilter
Op. 12, No. 1

Poco andante (♩ = 56)

Weep you no more, sad foun - tains; What need you flow so fast? Look how the snow - y moun - tains Heav'n's sun doth gent - ly

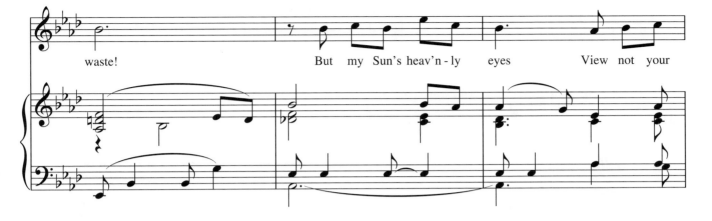

waste! But my Sun's heav'n-ly eyes View not your

weep - ing, That now lies sleep - ing,

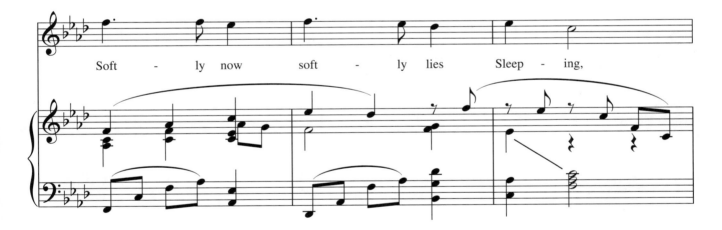

Soft - ly now soft - ly lies Sleep - ing,

sleep - ing.

Ped. *

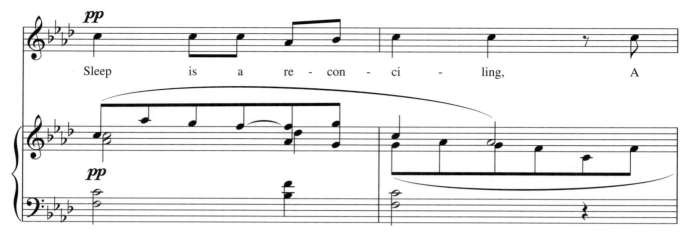

Sleep is a re-con-ci - ling, A

rest that peace be - gets;

Doth not the sun rise smi - ling When

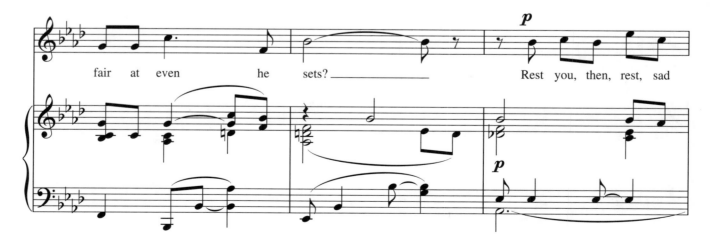

fair at even he sets? _____ Rest you, then, rest, sad

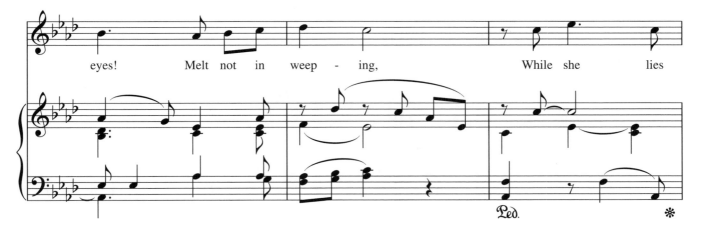

eyes! Melt not in weep - ing, While she lies

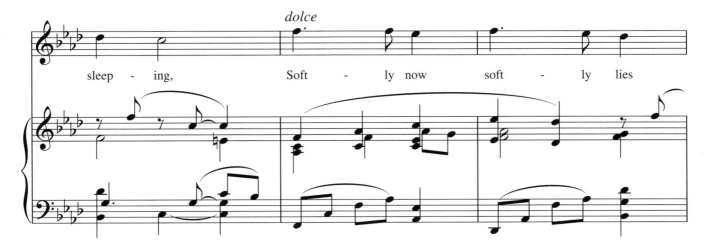

dolce

sleep - ing, Soft - ly now soft - ly lies

Sleep - ing, sleep - ing.

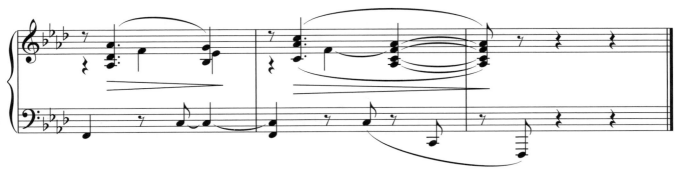

1:31

To the memory of my friend, Mrs. Cary-Elwes

MY LIFE'S DELIGHT

from Seven Elizabethan Songs, Op. 12

original key

Words by
Thomas Campion

Music by
Roger Quilter
Op. 12, No. 2

Molto allegro con moto (♩ = 132)

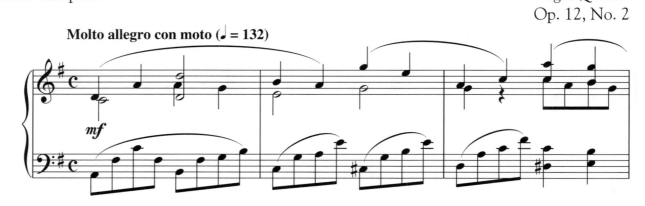

Come, O come, my life's de - light!

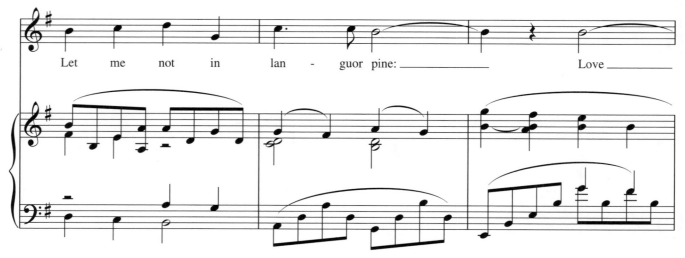

Let me not in lan - guor pine: _____ Love _____

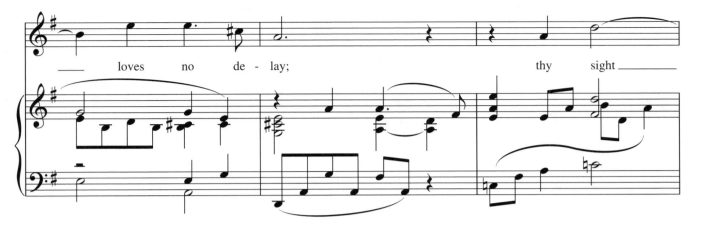

loves no de - lay; thy sight _____

poco cresc.

_____ The more en - joyed, the more di - vine. O come, _____

poco rall.

_____ O come, and take from me The pain of being de - priv'd of

poco rall.

thee.

poco rit.

mf a tempo

Thou all sweet - ness dost en - close,

Like a lit - tle world of bliss: Beau - ty, beau -

- ty guards thy looks: the rose _____

_____ In them pure and e - ter - nal is. Come

then, come then! O come, and make thy

flight As swift, as _____ swift to me

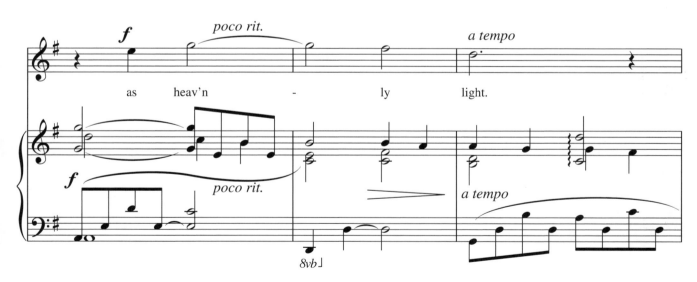

as heav'n - ly light.

To the memory of my friend, Mrs. Cary-Elwes

DAMASK ROSES

from Seven Elizabethan Songs, Op. 12

original key

Words Anonymous

Music by
Roger Quilter
Op. 12, No. 3

har - bours, My eyes pre - sent me with a dou - ble doubt - ing:

opt.

For view - ing both a - like, hard - ly my mind sup -

L.H.

espressivo *poco rit.*

po - ses Wheth-er the ro - ses be your lips, or your lips the

poco rit.
colla voce

ro - ses.

mf *lento con espressione* *pp*

To the memory of my friend, Mrs. Cary-Elwes

BROWN IS MY LOVE
from Seven Elizabethan Songs, Op. 12
original key

Words Anonymous

Music by
Roger Quilter
Op. 12, No. 5

Poco andante grazioso con tenerezza (♩ = 58)

Brown is my Love, but grace - ful, And
each re - nown - ed white - ness, Match'd with her love - ly
brown, lo - seth its bright - ness;

cantabile

To the memory of my friend, Mrs. Cary-Elwes

BY A FOUNTAINSIDE

from Seven Elizabethan Songs, Op. 12

original key

Words by
Ben Jonson

Music by
Roger Quilter
Op. 12, No. 6

Slow, slow, fresh fount, keep time with my salt tears; Yet

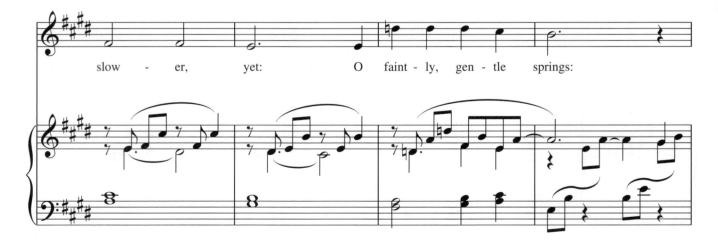

slow - er, yet: O faint - ly, gen - tle springs:

List to the hea- vy part _____ the mu- sic bears, _____

Woe weeps out her di- vi- sion when she sings,

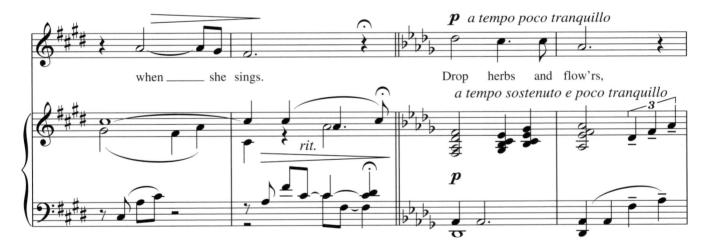

when _____ she sings.

p *a tempo poco tranquillo*

Drop herbs and flow'rs,

a tempo sostenuto e poco tranquillo

rit.

p

cresc.

Fall grief in show'rs, Our beau- ties are not ours; _____

cresc.

poco con moto

f

Ped.

To the memory of my friend, Mrs. Cary-Elwes

FAIR HOUSE OF JOY

from Seven Elizabethan Songs, Op. 12

original key

Words Anonymous

Music by
Roger Quilter
Op. 12, No. 7

rote, Fan-cy-ing that that harm'd me: Yet when this thought doth

poco cresc.

come "Love, _____ Love is the per-fect sum Of all de-

light!" I have no oth - er choice Ei - ther for pen or

voice To sing or write.

dolce amoroso

O Love! they wrong thee much That say thy

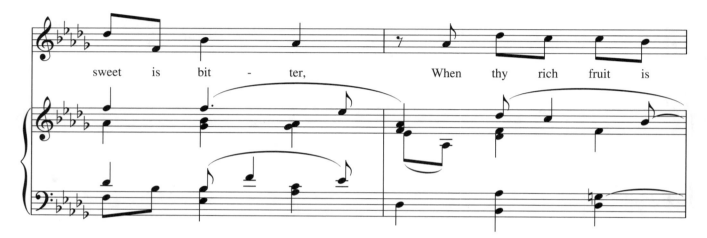

sweet is bit - ter, When thy rich fruit is

such As no - thing can be sweet - er.

cresc.

Fair house of joy and bliss, Where tru - est, where tru - est plea - sure

To Robin and Aimée Legge

AUTUMN EVENING

from Four Songs, Op. 14

original key: G minor

Words by
Arthur Maquarie

Music by
Roger Quilter
Op. 14, No. 1

Moderato tranquillo (♩ = 58)

mp *sostenuto e cantabile*

mp

The yel-low pop-lar leaves have

strown Thy qui-et mound, thou slum-ber-est

Where win-ter's winds will be un-known; So

deep thy rest, _____ so deep thy rest _____

poco rit.

a tempo

pp

Sleep on, my love, thy dreams are sweet,

If thou hast dreams; the flow'rs I brought

poco cresc.

112

To Robin and Aimée Legge

APRIL

from Four Songs, Op. 14

original key: A-flat Major

Words by
William Watson

Music by
Roger Quilter
Op. 14, No. 2

A - pril, that mine ears Like a lov - er

greet - est, If I tell thee, sweet - est, All my hopes and

cresc.

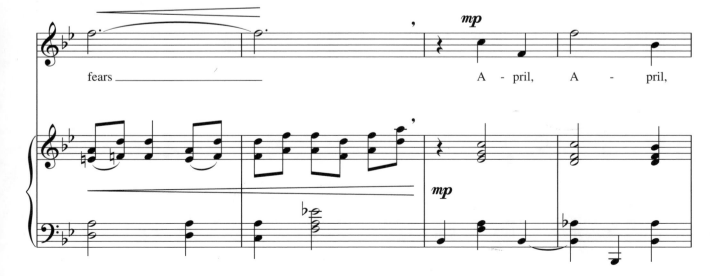

fears A - pril, A - pril,

mp

Laugh thy gol-den laugh - ter, But, the mo - ment af - ter

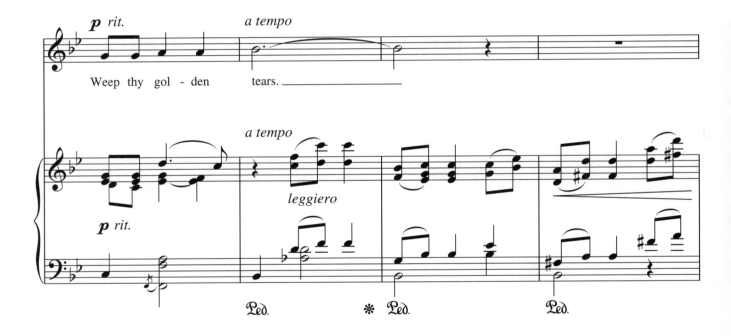

Weep thy gol - den tears. _____

To Robin and Aimée Legge

A LAST YEAR'S ROSE

from Four Songs, Op. 14

original key: D-flat Major

Words by
W.E. Henley

Music by
Roger Quilter
Op. 14, No. 3

Lyrics:

From the brake the Night - in - gale Sings _ ex - ult - ing to the Rose;

Though he sees her wax - ing pale In her pas - sion - ate re -

pose _____ While she tri - umphs wax - ing frail,

Fa - ding, fa - ding ev - en while she glows;___ Though he knows ___

How it goes _____ Knows of last year's Night - in - gale,

Dead with last year's Rose.

Wise the en-a-moured Night - in - gale, Wise _ the well - be - lov - ed Rose!

Love and life shall still pre - vail, Nor the si - lence, the

si - lence at the close _____ Break the ma - gic of the

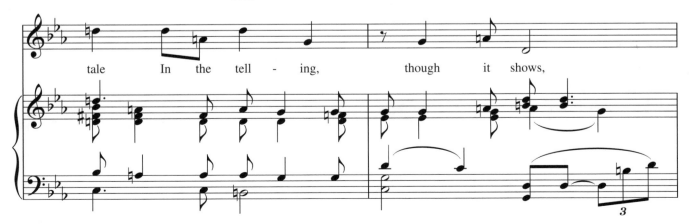

tale In the tell - ing, though it shows,

To Robin and Aimée Legge

SONG OF THE BLACKBIRD

from Four Songs, Op. 14

original key

Words by
W.E. Henley

Music by
Roger Quilter
Op. 14, No. 4

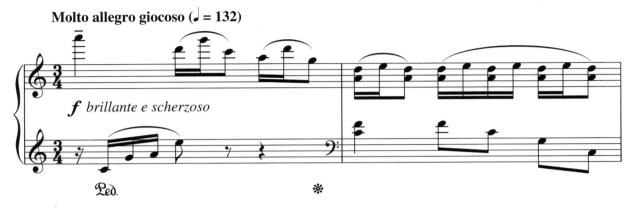

Molto allegro giocoso (♩ = 132)

f brillante e scherzoso

Ped.

un poco meno allegro ma con spirito

The Night - in - gale ___ has a

lyre of gold, The Lark's is a cla - rion call, And the

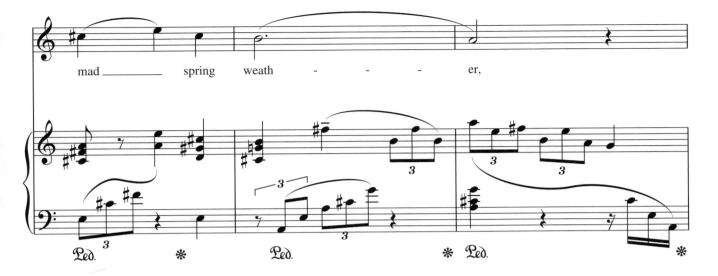

mad _____ spring weath - - - er,

molto cresc.

We two have lis - tened till he sang _____

mp *cresc.* *molto cresc.*

f appassionato *allargando*

Our hearts _____ and

f

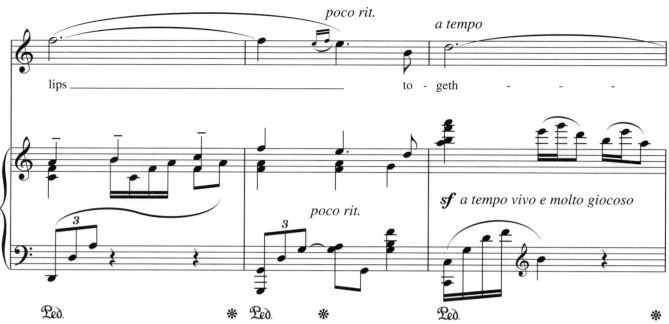

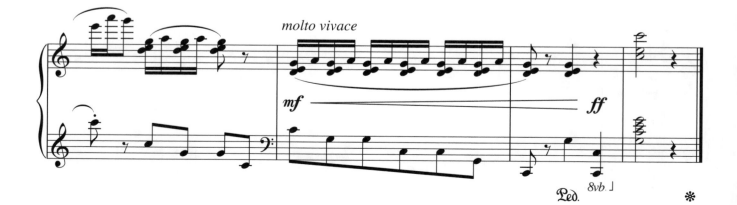

To Theodore Byard

TO WINE AND BEAUTY

from Six Songs, Op. 18

original key: E-flat Major

Words by
the Earl of Rochester,
Seventeenth Century

Music by
Roger Quilter
Op. 18, No. 1

Moderato ma con moto ed appassionato ($\quarternote$ = 90)

Vul - can pro - vide me such a cup As Nes - tor used of

old: Try all your art to trim it up And

poco rit.

dam-ask it round with gold.

poco rit.

Ped. ✳

a tempo
con amore
mp

Carve me there on a curl-ing vine, A love-ly girl and

a tempo

mp

Ped. ✳ Ped. ✳

boy: Their limbs in am'-rous folds en-twine, The

type of fu-ture joy. Make it so large, when

f

gioioso

f

Ped. ✳ Ped. ✳

wine   we'll   drive   a - way   all   care, _____ And then to

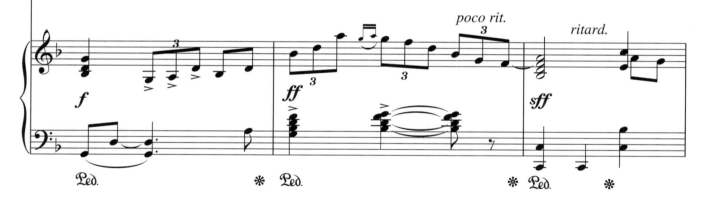

Love _____ to   Love _____ a -

gain. _____

to H. Plunket Greene

WHERE BE YOU GOING?

from Six Songs, Op. 18

original key: D Major

Words by
John Keats

Music by
Roger Quilter
Op. 18, No. 2

Moderato semplice (♩ = 60)

delicato e giocoso

dolce

Where be you go - ing, you Dev - on maid? And

what have ye there in the bask - et? Ye tight lit - tle fair - y, just

fresh from the dai - ry, Will you give me some cream if I

ask it? I love your hills and I love your dales, And I

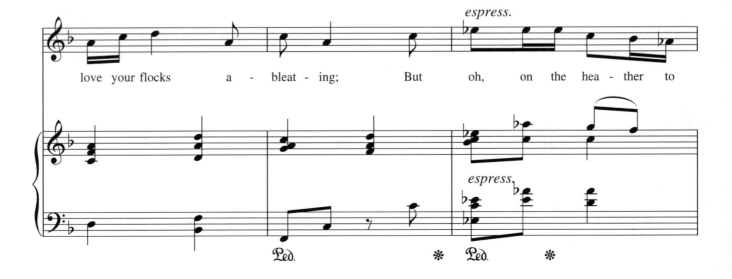

love your flocks a - bleat - ing; But oh, on the hea - ther to

lie to-geth - er, With both our hearts, our hearts _____ a-

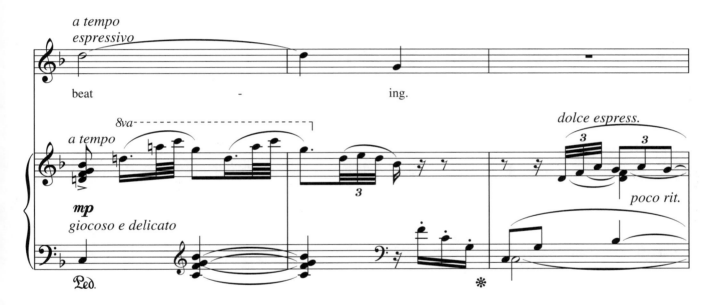

beat - ing.

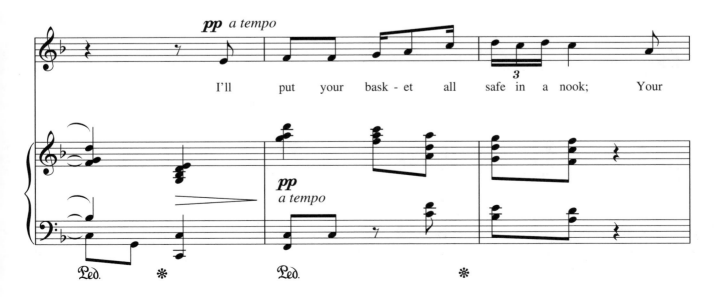

I'll put your bask - et all safe in a nook; Your

shawl I'll hang ____ on a wil - low; And we will sigh in the

dai - sy's eye, And kiss on a grass - green

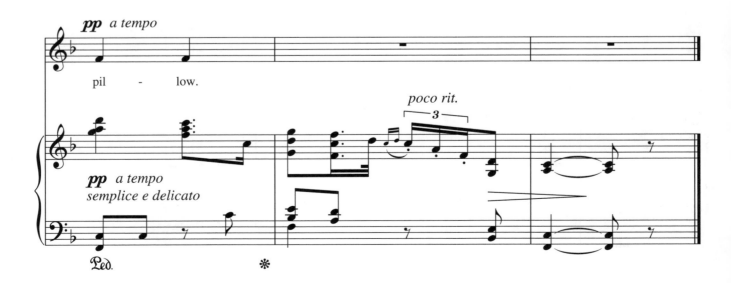

pil - low.

to Frederic Austin

THE JOCUND DANCE

from Six Songs, Op. 18

original key: G Major

Words by
William Blake

Music by
Roger Quilter
Op. 18, No. 3

in - no - cent eyes do glance, And where lisps, where

lisps the maid - en's tongue. I love the laugh - ing

vale, I love the ech - oing hill, _____ Where

mirth does nev - er ___ fail, And the jol - ly swain, the

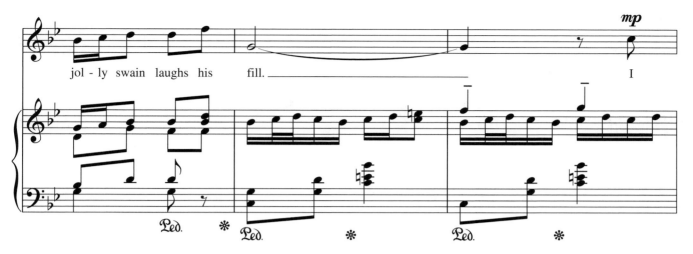

jol - ly swain laughs his fill. _____ I

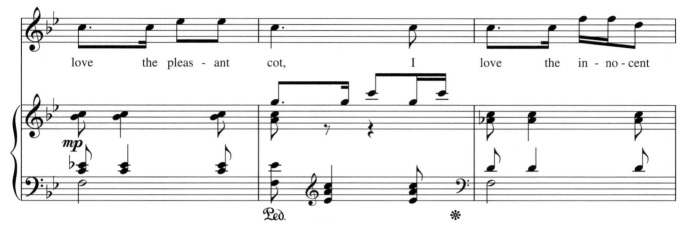

love the pleas - ant cot, I love the in - no - cent

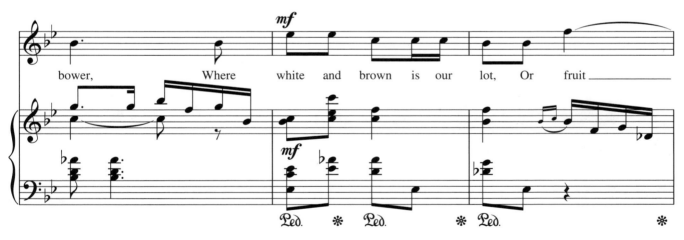

bower, Where white and brown is our lot, Or fruit _____

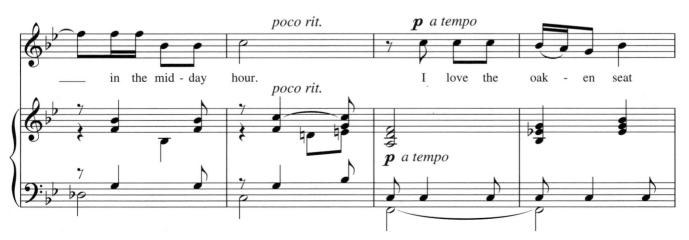

_____ in the mid - day hour. I love the oak - en seat

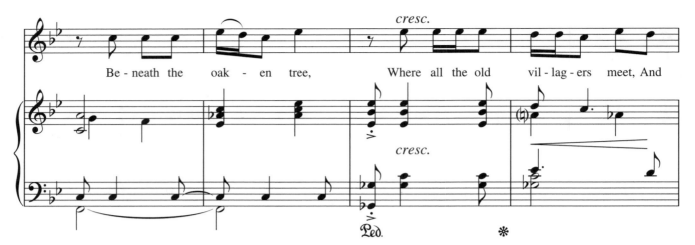

Be - neath the oak - en tree, Where all the old vil - lag - ers meet, And

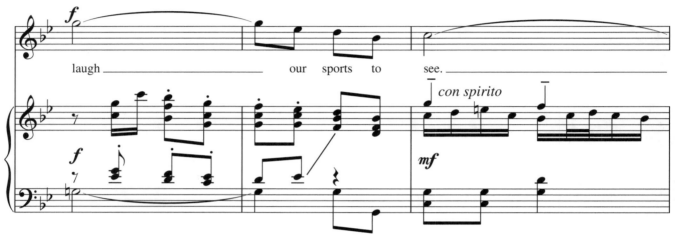

laugh _____ our sports to see. _____

I love our neigh - bours all,— But,

to Madame Kirkby Lunn

THE SPRING IS AT THE DOOR

from Six Songs, Op. 18

original key: D Major

Words by
Nora Hopper

Music by
Roger Quilter
Op. 18, No. 4

The Spring is at the door: She bears a gold-en store, Her maund with yel-low daf-fo-dils run-neth o'er ___ Her

139

maund with yel - low daf - fo - dils run - neth o'er. ____ Her

ro - sy feet are bare, The wind is in her hair, And

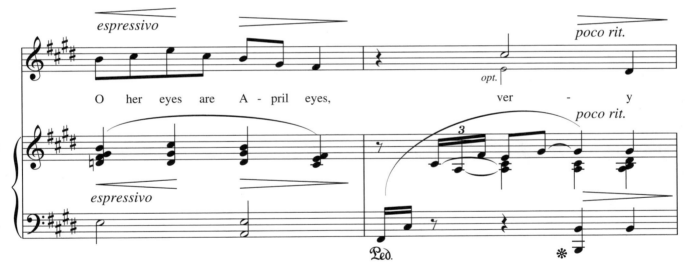

O her eyes are A - pril eyes, ver - y

fair.

To Miss Muriel Foster

THROUGH THE SUNNY GARDEN

from Two September Songs, Op. 18

original key: E Major

Words by
Mary Coleridge

Music by
Roger Quilter
Op. 18, No. 5

Andante moderato (♩ = 42)

Through the sun - ny gar - den The hum - mimg bees are

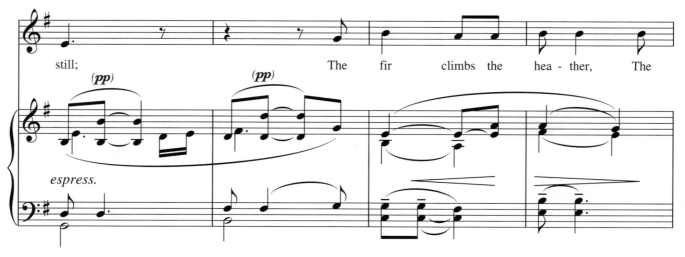

still; The fir climbs the hea - ther, The

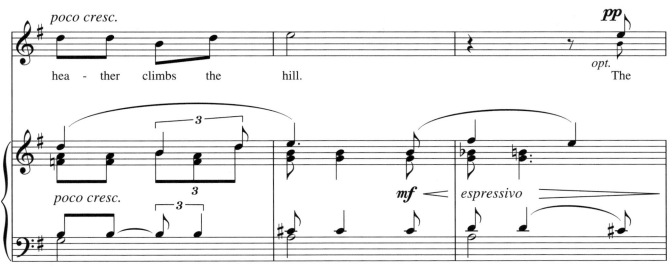

hea- ther climbs the hill. The

low clouds have ri - ven A lit - tle rift

through._____ The hill climbs to heav - en,

To Miss Muriel Foster

THE VALLEY AND THE HILL

from Two September Songs, Op. 18

original key: D minor

Words by
Mary Coleridge

Music by
Roger Quilter
Op. 18, No. 6

Allegro con moto e poco appassionato (♩ = 138)

O the high val - ley, the lit - tle low hill. And the corn - field o - ver the sea, _____ The wind that ra - ges and then lies still, And the

clouds that rest and flee!

O the gray is-land in the rain-bow haze, And the long thin spits of

land, ___ The rough-'ning pas-tures and the sto-ny ways, And the

gold-en flash of the sand! ___

To my friend, Florence Koehler

DREAM VALLEY
from Three Songs of William Blake, Op. 20
original key: D Major

Words by
William Blake

Music by
Roger Quilter
Op. 20, No. 1

To my friend, Florence Koehler

THE WILD FLOWER'S SONG
from Three Songs of William Blake, Op. 20

original key: G Major

Words by
William Blake

Music by
Roger Quilter
Op. 20 No. 2

ma tranquillo
p
slept in the earth In the si-lent night; I mur - mured my thoughts, And I
a tempo ma tranquillo
pp
p
Ped. *
p poco a poco più mosso e crescendo
felt de - light. In the morn - ing I went, As ro - sy as morn,
poco a poco più mosso e crescendo
p
Ped. * Ped. * Ped. * Ped. *
poco rit.
f
poco più lento ed espress.
mp
To seek for new joy, But I met with
f
poco largamente e rit.
dim.
poco più lento
Ped. * Ped. *
scorn."
a tempo
molto espress. e poco rit.
mp
mp
mf
Ped. * Ped. * Ped. *

As I wan-dered in the for-est The green leaves a-mong,

I heard a wild flower sing - ing, _____ sing - ing,

sing - ing a song. _____

To my friend, Florence Koehler

DAYBREAK

from Three Songs of William Blake, Op. 20

original key: E-flat minor

Words by
William Blake

Music by
Roger Quilter
Op. 20, No. 3

Tempo moderato (♩ = 72) ma con moto e poco rubato

To find the west - ern path, Right through the gates of wrath I urge my way; *poco rit.* Sweet morn - ing leads me on; With soft re -

più tranquillo
mp dolce
più tranquillo

ma a tempo

The sun is freed from fears, And with soft grate - ful tears As - cends the sky.

To Monica Harrison

I WILL GO WITH MY FATHER A-PLOUGHING

from Three Pastoral Songs, Op. 22

original key: A-flat Major

Words by
Joseph Campbell

Music by
Roger Quilter
Op. 22, No. 1

red field by __ the sea, And the rooks and the gulls and the

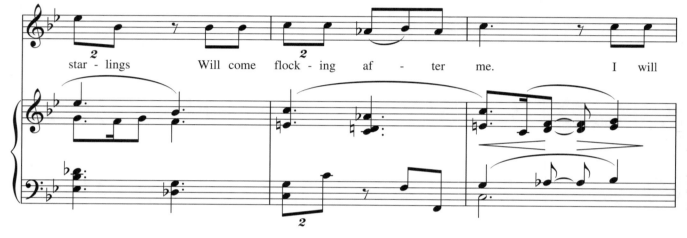

star - lings Will come flock - ing af - ter me. I will

sing to the strid - ing sow - ers With the finch on the flow'r - ing

sloe, And my fa - ther will sing the seed - song __

160

To Monica Harrison

CHERRY VALLEY

from Three Pastoral Songs, Op. 22

original key: E Major

Words by
Joseph Campbell

Music by
Roger Quilter
Op. 22, No. 2

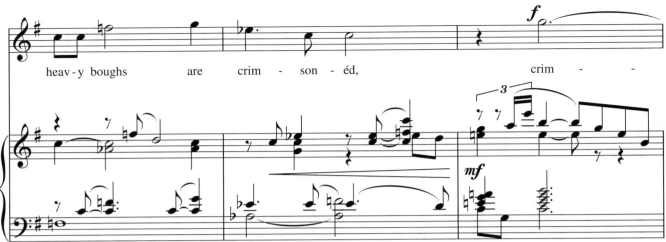

heav-y boughs   are   crim - son - éd,   crim -

- son - éd.

poco cresc.

f

rit.

Now the low moon is look-ing through _____ The glim - mer   of the

p a tempo

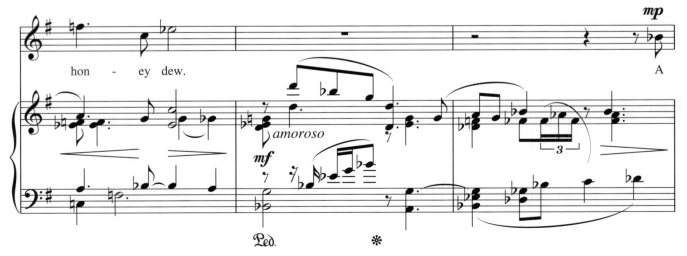

hon - ey dew.   A

amoroso

mf

pet - al trem-bles to the grass,____ The feet of fai - ries

pass _____ and pass.

In Cher ry Val - ley the cher ries blow; The val - ley paths are white as snow;

white as snow.____

To Monica Harrison

I WISH AND I WISH

from Three Pastoral Songs, Op. 22

original key: C minor/C Major

Words by
Joseph Campbell

Music by
Roger Quilter
Op. 22, No. 3

Allegro moderato ma con moto (♩. = 84)

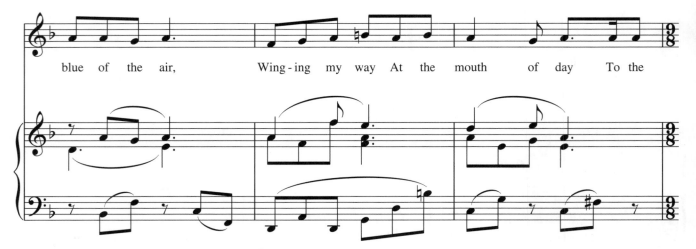

I wish and I wish And I wish I were A gold - en bee In the

blue of the air, Wing - ing my way At the mouth of day To the

honey marges Of Loch Kyoon bawn;* Or a little green drake, Or a silver swan, Floating upon The stream of Aili, And I to be swimming Gaily, gaily.

poco rit. rall. p dolce

I

*Loch-ciuin-ban—"The fair, calm lake."

*Magh-meala—"The plain of honey"

To Walter Creighton

UNDER THE GREENWOOD TREE

from Five Shakespeare Songs, Op. 23 (Second Set)

original key: D Major

Words by
William Shakespeare
from *As You Like It*

Music by
Roger Quilter
Op. 23, No. 2

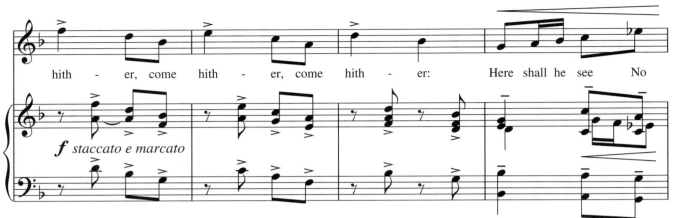

hith - er, come hith - er, come hith - er:　Here shall he see　No

en - em - y　But　win - ter and rough weath - er.

Who　doth am - bi - tion

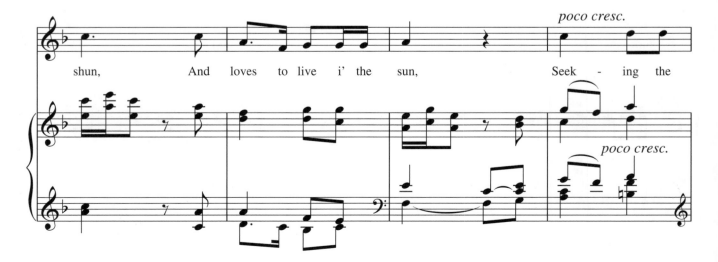

shun,　And　loves to live i' the sun,　Seek - ing the

To the memory of Robin Hollway

FEAR NO MORE THE HEAT O' THE SUN

from Five Shakespeare Songs, Op. 23 (Second Set)

original key: F minor

Words by
William Shakespeare
from *Cymbeline*

Music by
Roger Quilter
Op. 23, No. 1

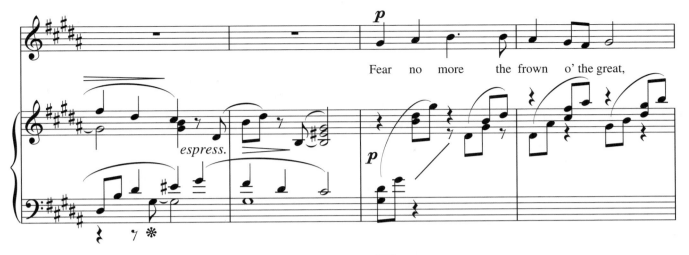

Fear no more the frown o' the great,

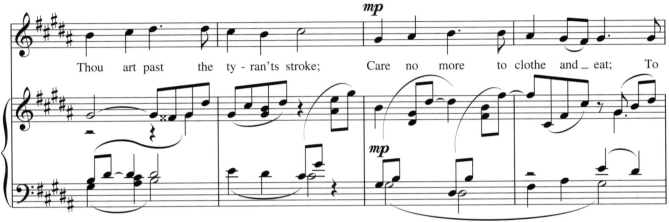

Thou art past the ty-ran's stroke; Care no more to clothe and _ eat; To

thee the reed is as _ the oak: The scep-tre, learn-ing, phy-sic, must All

fol-low this, and come to dust.

To Walter Creighton

IT WAS A LOVER AND HIS LASS

from Five Shakespeare Songs, Op. 23 (Second Set)

original key: E Major

Words by
William Shakespeare
from *As You Like It*

Music by
Roger Quilter
Op. 23, No. 3

was a lov-er and his lass, With a hey, and a ho, And a hey no-ni-no, That o'er the green corn-field did pass, In the spring time, the on-ly

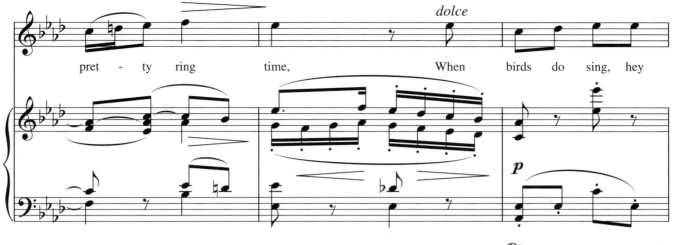

pret - ty ring time, When birds do sing, hey

ding a ding, ding, ding a dung, ding, ding a ding, ding; Sweet

lov - ers love _ the spring. _____ Be -

tween the a - cres of the rye, With a hey, and a ho, and a hey no - ni - no, These

poco ten. *a tempo*

pret - ty coun - try folks would lie, In the apring time,

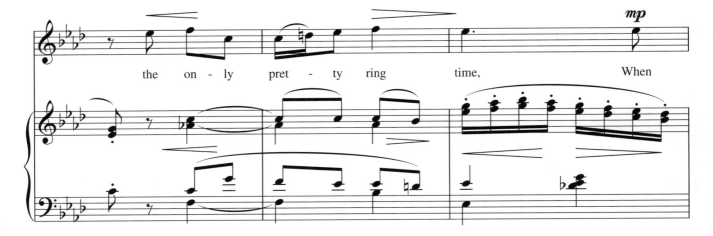

the on - ly pret - ty ring time, When

birds do sing, hey ding a ding, ding, ding a ding, ding, ding a ding, ding; Sweet

lov - ers love _ the spring. _ This

pochiss. riten. *mf*

lov - ers love _ the spring. _____ And

pochiss. riten.

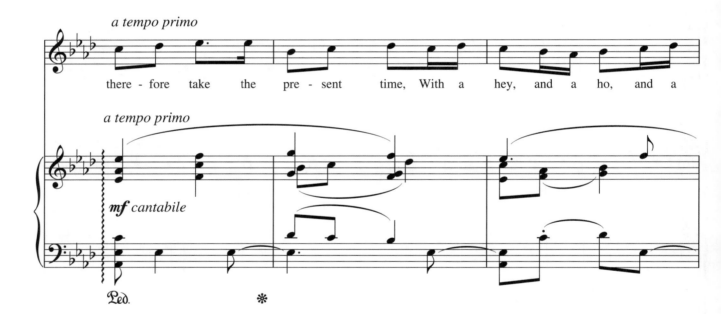

a tempo primo

there - fore take the pre - sent time, With a hey, and a ho, and a

a tempo primo

mf cantabile

Ped. *

poco riten. *mp* *a tempo*

hey no - ni - no, For love _ is crown - éd with the _ prime In the spring time,

poco riten. *a tempo* *mp*

the on - ly pret - ty ring time, When

mp

birds do sing, hey ding a ding, ding, ding a ding, ding,

mp

ℒℯ𝒹. ✻ ℒℯ𝒹. ✻ ℒℯ𝒹. ✻

ritardando poco
ten.
p

ding a ding, ding; Sweet lov - ers love ___ the spring.

poco
ten.

p

8va

pp

ritardando

ℒℯ𝒹. ✻

To A.C. Landsberg

TAKE, O TAKE THOSE LIPS AWAY

from Five Shakespeare Songs, Op. 23 (Second Set)

original key: D-flat Major

Words by
William Shakespeare
from *Measure for Measure*

Music by
Roger Quilter
Op. 23, No. 4

morn: But my kiss - es bring a - gain,

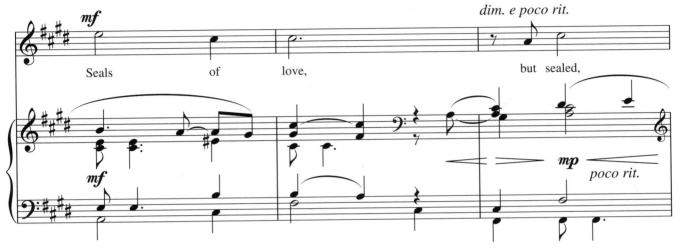

Seals of love, but sealed,

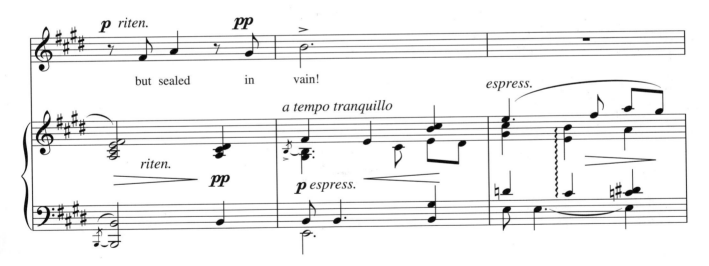

but sealed in vain!

To Walter Creighton

HEY, HO, THE WIND AND THE RAIN

from Five Shakespeare Songs, Op. 23 (Second Set)

original key: C major

Words by
William Shakespeare
from *Twelfth Night*

Music by
Roger Quilter
Op. 23, No. 5

day. _____ But when I came to

mp

giocoso

p

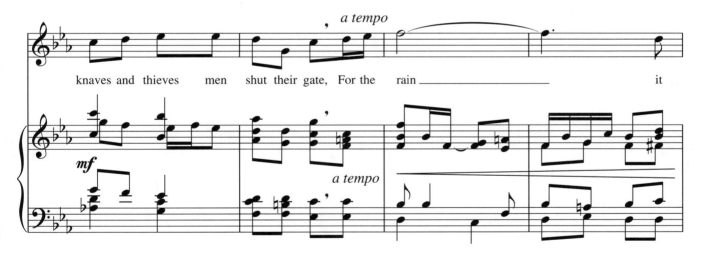

man's es - tate, With hey, ho, the wind and the rain; 'Gainst

mf

stacc. *mp*

knaves and thieves men shut their gate, For the rain _____ it

a tempo

mf

a tempo

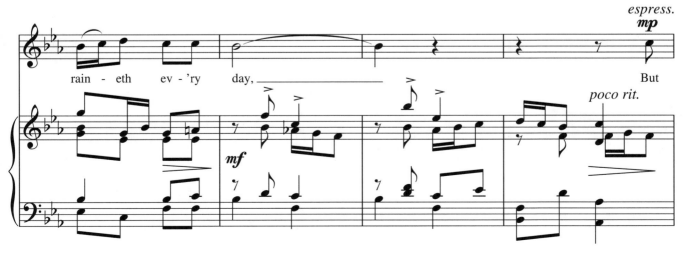

rain - eth ev - 'ry day, _____ But

espress.
mp

poco rit.

mf

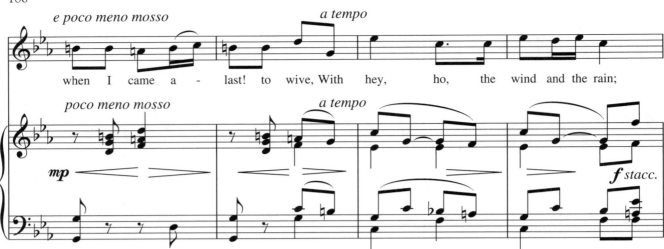

e poco meno mosso   *a tempo*

when I came a - last! to wive, With hey, ho, the wind and the rain;

poco meno mosso   *a tempo*

By swag-ger-ing could I nev - er thrive, _____ For the

rain _____ it rain - eth ev - 'ry day _____

Più moderato
poco ten.

pochiss. rit.

A

great while a - go the world be - gun, With hey, ho, the winds and the rain;

But that's all one, our play is done, And we'll strive, _____ we'll

strive to please you ev - 'ry day. _____

To Louis and Dinah de Glehn

IN THE HIGHLANDS

from Two Songs, Op. 26

original key: E-flat Major

Words by
Robert Louis Stevenson

Music by
Roger Quilter
Op. 26, No. 1

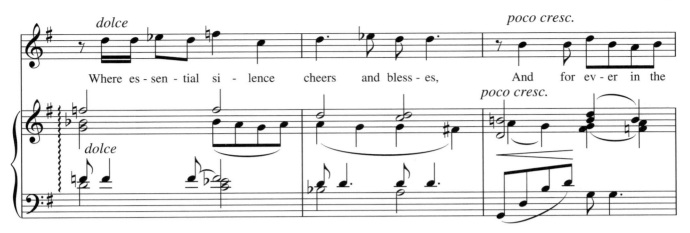

dolce .... *poco cresc.*

Where es - sen - tial si - lence cheers and bless - es, And for ev - er in the

hill - re - cess - es Her more love - ly mu - sic _____ Broods and

dies. _____

O to mount a - gain where erst I haunt - ed; _____ Where the old red hills are

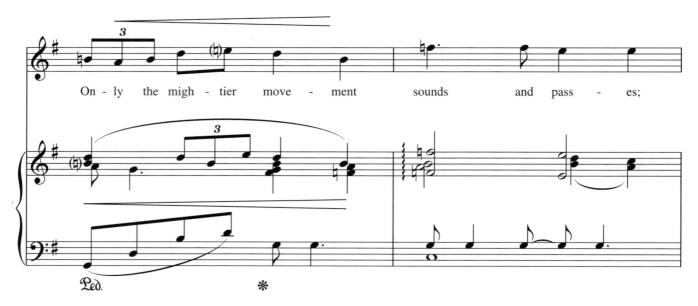

On - ly the migh - tier move - ment sounds and pass - es;

espress.

On - ly winds and riv - ers, _____ Life and death.

espress.

p dolce tranquillo

poco rit.

pp

ppp

8vb

To Louis and Dinah de Glehn

OVER THE LAND IS APRIL

from Two Songs, Op. 26

original key: C Major

Words by
Robert Louis Stevenson

Music by
Roger Quilter
Op. 26, No. 2

Allegro appassionato ($\unicode{x2669} = 76$)

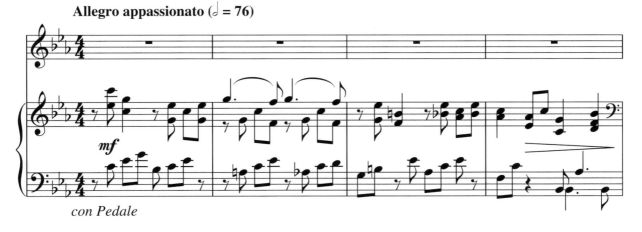

con Pedale

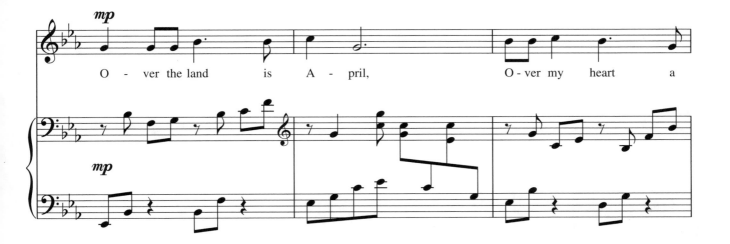

O - ver the land is A - pril, O - ver my heart a

rose; O - ver the high, brown moun - tain

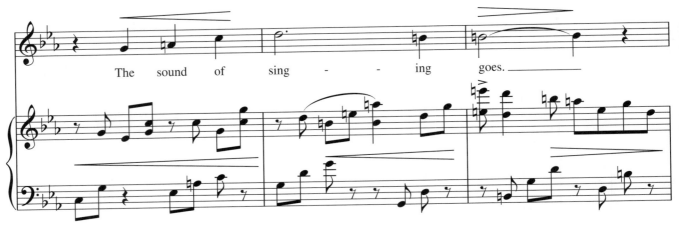

The sound of sing - - ing goes.

Say, love, do you hear me, Hear my son-nets ring?

O - ver the high, brown moun - tain, Love, do you hear me

sing? By

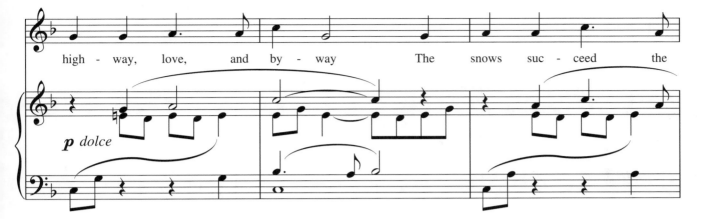

high - way, love, and by - way The snows suc - ceed the

p dolce

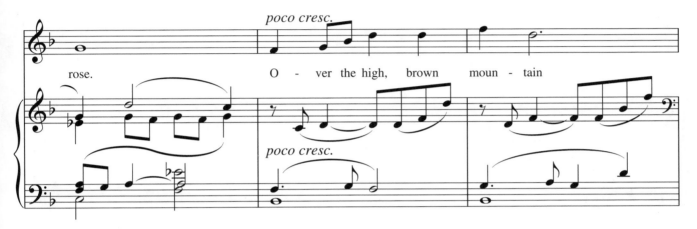

rose. O - ver the high, brown moun - tain

poco cresc.

poco cresc.

The wind of win - - - ter blows. _____

p

Say, love, do you hear me, Hear my son - nets

p

cresc.

ring? O - ver the high, brown moun - tain

I sound the song of spring.

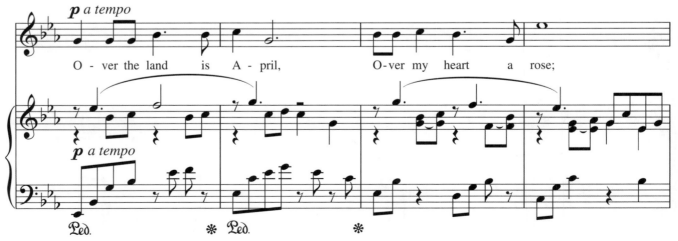

p a tempo

O - ver the land is A - pril, O - ver my heart a rose;

O - ver the high, brown moun - tain   The sound of

sing - - ing goes. _____   Say, love, do you

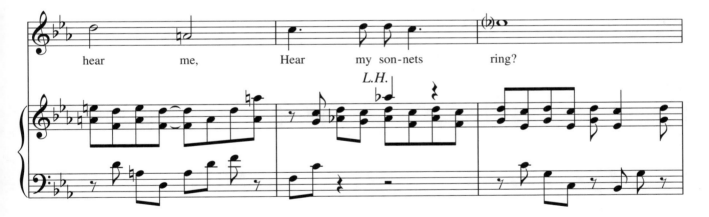

hear   me,   Hear   my son-nets   ring?

O - ver the high, brown moun - tain,   Love,   do you

For Frederick Ranalow

BARBARA ALLEN

from *Old English Popular Songs*

original key: D Major

Words Anonymous

old English melody
arranged by
Roger Quilter

Moderato, poco con moto (♩ = 72)

espressivo

In Scar - let Town, where I was born, There was a fair maid dwell-in', Made ev'-ry youth cry __ "Well - a - day!" Her name was Bar - b'ra Al - len. All in the mer - ry

dolce e grazioso

delicato e grazioso

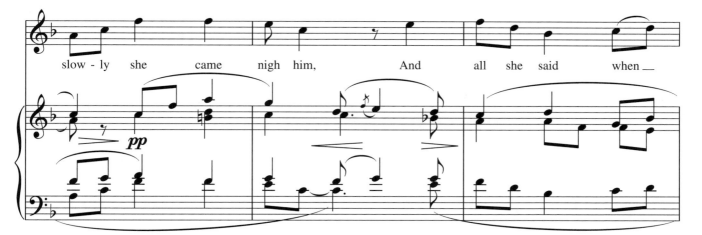

slow - ly she came nigh him, And all she said when __

poco accel.

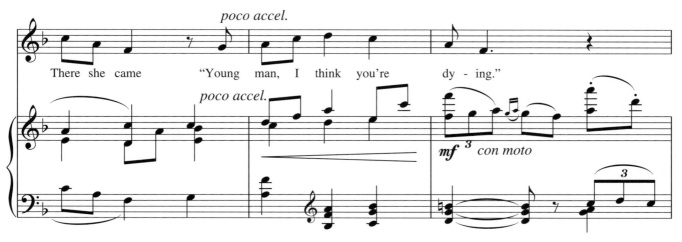

There she came "Young man, I think you're dy - ing."

mf 3 con moto

sonoro
mp

poco dim. *pochiss. rit.* As

she was walk - ing o'er the fields She heard the dead - bell

mp sonoro

L.H. *p* *sf*

Ped.

For Arthur Frith

DRINK TO ME ONLY WITH THINE EYES

from *Old English Popular Songs*

original key: E-flat Major

Words by
Ben Jonson

English Air by Colonel Mellish
arranged by
Roger Quilter

For Joseph Farrington

THE JOLLY MILLER

from *Old English Popular Songs*

original key: G minor

Words Anonymous
from *Love in a Village*, 1762

old English melody
arranged by
Roger Quilter

this the bur - den of his song For ev - er used to

be _____ I care for no - bod - y, no, not I, if

no - bod - y cares for me. _____

molto giocoso

love my mill, she is to me Both par - ent, child and

wife; _____ I would not change my sta - tion for An -

oth - er one in life. _____ Then _ push, push, push the

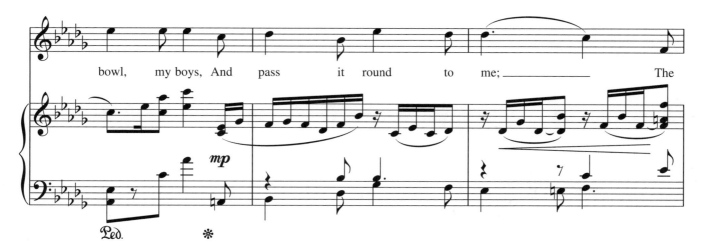

bowl, my boys, And pass it round to me; _____ The

long - er we ___ sit here and drink The mer - ri - er we shall

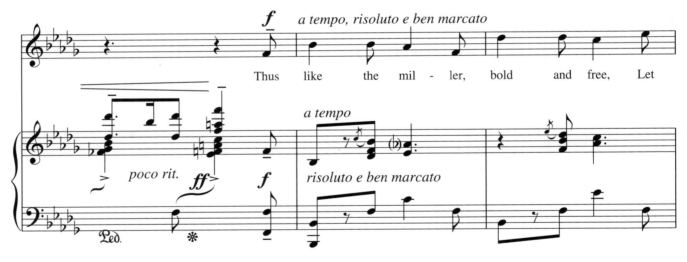

be. ___

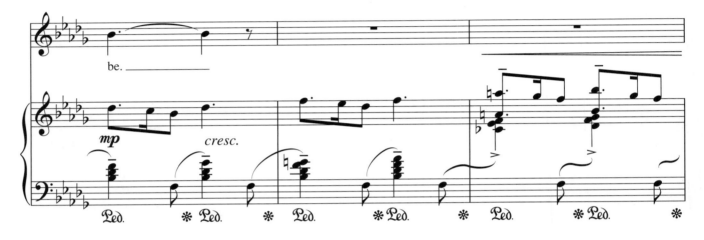

Thus like the mil - ler, bold and free, Let

us re - joice and sing. ___ The days of youth were made for glee And

For Theodore Byard

OVER THE MOUNTAINS

from *Old English Popular Songs*

original key

Words from
Thomas Percy's
collection of ballads
Reliques

Air from *Musick's Recreation on
the Lyra Viol*, 1652
arranged by
Roger Quilter

Allegro con moto (♩ = 144)

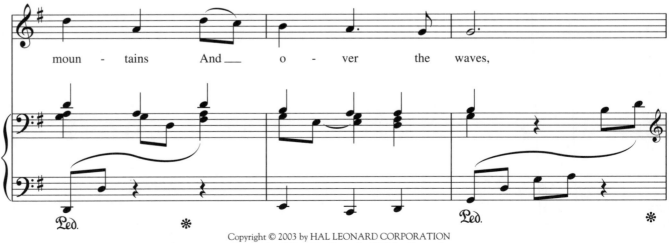

Un - der the ___ foun - tains And ___ un - der the

graves, Un - der floods ___ that are deep - est Which ___

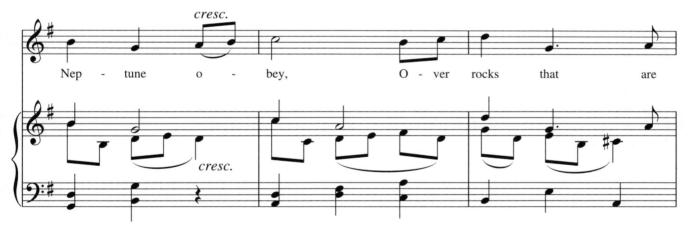

cresc.

Nep - tune o - bey, O - ver rocks that are

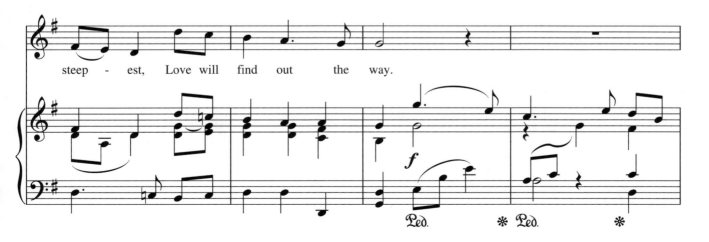

steep - est, Love will find out the way.

Where there is — no place For the

glow - worm to lie, Where there is — no space For re -

ceipt of a fly: Where the midge — dare not ven - ture Lest her -

self fast she — lay, If — Love come he will en - ter And will

find out the way.

Some think to — lose him Or — have him con -

fined. Some so sup - pose him, Poor — thing, to be

blind; But if ne'er so close ye wall him, Do the best that ye —

may, Blind __ Love, if so ye call __ him, Soon will

find out his way.

You may train the eag - le To __

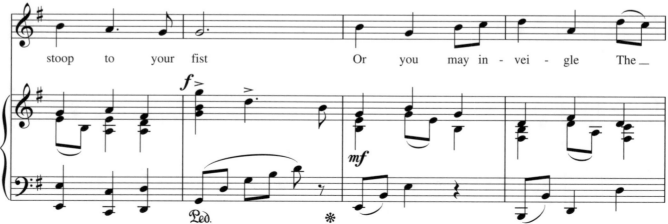

stoop to your fist Or you may in - vei - gle The __

phoen - ix of the East. The ___ lion - ess you may move her To ___ get o'er her ___ prey, But you'll ne'er stop a lov - er, Love shall find out the way. ___

For Guy Vivian

THREE POOR MARINERS

from *Old English Popular Songs*

original key: E-flat Major

Words and Air from Freeman's Songs
in *Deuteromelia*, 1609

arranged by
Roger Quilter

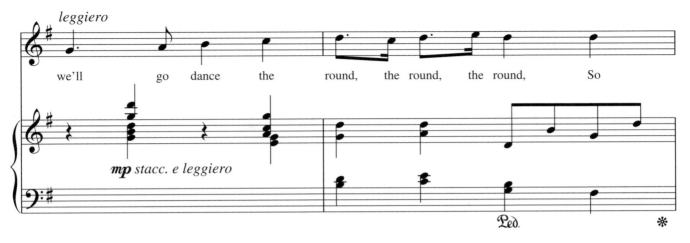

leggiero

we'll go dance the round, the round, the round, So

mp *stacc. e leggiero*

mf

we'll_ go dance the round,_____ And he that is a

mf

bul- ly, bul- ly boy Come pledge me on the ground, the ground, the ground.

f

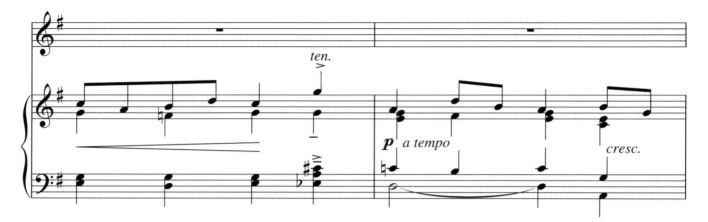

Maestoso e poco più moderato

We care not for those mar - tial men That

do ___ our states dis - dain, But we care for those

mar - chant men ___ Who do our states main - tain. So

Notes on the Songs

Three Songs of the Sea, Op. 1

The Sea-Bird
Moonlight
By the Sea

Composed 1900. In its original form, the set was *Four Songs of the Sea*. First performed at the Crystal Palace, London, March 11, 1901, by baritone Denham Price and Quilter as pianist. Published by Forsyth Bros. Quilter revised the text (by RQ) and music for a 1911 edition, eliminating the song "I Have a Friend." The songs were dedicated to the composer's mother, Lady Mary Quilter (b. 1840, d. 1927); mother and son were particularly devoted to one another.

Two Songs (1903)

Come Back!
A Secret

"A Secret" was composed in 1898; "Come Back!" probably dates from the same year. Published by Elkin, 1903. Withdrawn by the composer in 1915.

from Three Songs, Op. 3

Quilter designated these as Op. 3, though the songs were apparently not composed as a set.

Love's Philosophy

Composed c1905. Probaby first performed by tenor Gervase Elwes, to whom the song is dedicated, with Quilter as pianist. Published by Boosey and Co., 1905. Published by Schott in German translation, 1924. Elwes (1866-1921) was a celebrated concert singer, and Quilter's favorite. Elwes' voice was not especially large, but was well-suited to recital. He sang with clarity, finesse and sensitivity. This is one of the most recorded of Quilter songs. Recordings include those by John Aler, Arleen Auger, Janet Baker, Gervase Elwes, Elizabeth Harwood, Felicity Lott, John McCormack, Peter Pears, Rosa Ponselle, Joan Sutherland, and others. Quilter recorded the song with baritone Mark Raphael in 1934, and with baritone Frederick Harvey in 1945; both recordings are included on the CD packaged with *Roger Quilter: His Life and Music* by Valerie Langfield, The Boydell Press, 2002.

Now sleeps the crimson petal

Composed 1897, one of Quilter's first songs. Revised c1904. Published by Boosey and Co., 1904. Further later revisions were made for a 1946 edition. This volume presents the 1904 version. Published by Schott in German translation, 1924. Possible first performance April 23, 1904, Bechstein Hall, London, tenor Gervase Elwes, Quilter at the piano. This is the most recorded Quilter song. Recordings include those by Thomas Allen, Ian Bostridge, Gervase Elwes, Kathleen Ferrier, John McCormack, Peter Pears, Paul Robeson, Robert White, and others.

June (1905)

Composed c1905. Published by Boosey and Co., 1905. Probably composed for and first performed by soprano Ada Crossley, to whom the song is dedicated.

from Four Child Songs, Op. 5

A Good Child
The Lampligher
Where Go the Boats?

Composed c1905. Published by Chappell, 1914. The last song of the set, "Foreign Children," was omitted from the current compilation due to its quite outdated British imperialist viewpoint. Quilter revised two of the songs, "A Good Child" and "Where Go the Boats?," for a 1945 Chappell edition. This volume presents the 1914 versions. The set was dedicated to Quilter's second oldest sister, Norah Blanche Quilter Vivian, mother to two young children at the time of composition.

Three Shakespeare Songs, Op. 6 (First Set)

Come away, death
O mistress mine
Blow, blow, thou winter wind

Composed 1905. Published as a set by Boosey and Co., 1905. Published by Schott in German translation, 1920s. The songs are linked by key, but are a carefully planned grouping rather than a song cycle. The set was dedicated to Quilter's close friend Walter Creighton (1878-1958), a singer in his youth and the artist who premiered Ralph Vaughan Williams' *Songs of Travel*. Quilter made arrangements of the songs for voice and piano trio, voice and piano quartet, and voice and orchestra. The songs have sometimes been used in productions of Shakespeare plays. The set and individual songs have been often recorded. An arrangement for voice and piano quartet of "Come away, death" was recorded by Quilter (piano) and baritone Mark Raphael in 1934, released on the CD packaged with *Roger Quilter: His Life and Music* by Valerie Langfield, The Boydell Press, 2002. Quilter also accompanies the other two songs from the set on the same CD. Other highlight recordings: "Come away, death" by Ian Bostridge; "O mistress mine" by Peter Pears and Benjamin Britten, Paul Robeson; "Blow, blow, thou winter wind" by Marian Anderson, Jan Peerce.

To Julia, Op. 8

Prelude
The Bracelet
The Maiden Blush
To Daisies
The Night Piece
Julia's Hair
Interlude
Cherry Ripe

Composed 1905 for tenor Gervase Elwes (see "Love's Philosophy"), who premiered the piece with Quilter on October 31, 1905, Aeolian Hall, London. Published by Boosey and Co., 1906. This is Quilter's only proper song cycle. The poems were chosen from the large Robert Herrick collection *Hesperides*, published in 1648. Quilter's 1936 light opera *Julia* probably bore no relation to the song cycle, except the composer's partiality to the name. Quilter later made an arrangement of the cycle for voice and piano quintet, and also one for voice and string quartet. The composer directed a 1923 recording of the latter arrangement, included on the CD packaged with Valerie Langfield's *Roger Quilter: His Life and Music*, The Boydell Press, 2002. Quilter also made violin and piano transcriptions of "To Daisies" (unpublished), "Julia's Hair" (published by Boosey and Co., 1919), and "Love Song to Julia" ("Cherry Ripe") (published by Boosey and Co., 1919). "Julia's Hair" was also transcribed for cello and piano (published by Boosey and Co., 1919).

Seven Elizabethan Lyrics, Op. 12

Weep you no more
My Life's Delight
Damask Roses
The Faithless Shepherdess
Brown is my love
By a Fountainside
Fair House of Joy

Composed 1907. First performance most likely by tenor Gervase Elwes (see "Love's Philosophy") and Quilter, November 17, 1908, Bechstein Hall, London. Published as a set by Boosey and Co., 1908. Quilter rejected two songs originally composed for the set and wrote two new songs before the premiere. The texts for these songs had been variously published in collections. The set was dedicated to the memory of Gervase Elwes' mother, Alice Cary-Elwes, who died in 1907. The set and its individual songs have been recorded by several artists; "Weep you no more" and "Fair House of Joy" are the most often recorded, the first by Elly Ameling and others, the latter by Kathleen Ferrier and others. Quilter arranged "Weep you no more" as a vocal duet in 1938. The composer made various arrangements of some songs of the set for voice and orchestra. "Weep you no more" was also arranged by the composer for women's chorus.

Four Songs, Op. 14

Autumn Evening
April
A Last Year's Rose
Song of the Blackbird

Composed 1909-1910. Published by Boosey and Co., 1910. In *Roger Quilter: His Life and Music*, author Valerie Langfield writes, based on viewing the composer's autobiographical notes, "…the opening notes of the last song were taken from those of a real blackbird that Quilter had heard. Just after finishing the manuscripts of 'Autumn Evening' and 'Song of the Blackbird,' he left them in a taxi. They were never found, and he 'had to think them all over again.'" "Song of the Blackbird" was recorded by Quilter and baritone Mark Raphael, included in the CD packaged with Langfield's book.

Six Songs, Op. 18

Three Songs for Baritone or Tenor:
To Wine and Beauty
Where be you going?
The Jocund Dance

The Spring is at the door

Two September Songs:
Through the sunny garden
The Valley and the Hill

Though grouped by the composer under the same opus number, these six songs are really of three distinctions. The first three are more a true set, composed in 1913. The fourth song, composed in 1914, is a separate entity; the last two songs, composed in 1916, are another set. The first four songs were published individually by Elkin, 1914; the first three were subsequently released as *Three Songs for Baritone or Tenor* in 1920. (The very title reveals something significant about the composer's liberal view about transposition of his songs.) *Two September Songs* were published as a set by Elkin, 1916. The composer's alternate title for "To Wine and Beauty," crossed out in the manuscript, was "Bacchus Song." It is dedicated to Theodore Byard, an actor friend. "The Jocund Dance" was dedicated to friend and composer Frederic Austin. Though there is no apparent record of performance, the final two songs of the opus were probably premiered by Muriel Foster, a singer to whom they were dedicated. "Where be you going?" was recorded by Quilter and baritone Mark Raphael, included in the CD packaged with *Roger Quilter: His Life and Music*, by Valerie Langfield, The Boydell Press, 2002.

Three Songs of William Blake, Op. 20

Dream Valley
The Wild Flower's Song
Daybreak

The first was composed in 1916, the remaining songs in 1917. First performed by Muriel Foster and Quilter, December 14, 1917, Wigmore Hall, London. Published by Winthrop Rogers, 1917.

Three Pastoral Songs, Op. 22

I will go with my father a-ploughing
Cherry Valley
I wish and I wish

Composed 1920. The set was originally scored for piano trio. Elkin published it in 1921 with and without string parts. Though the premiere performance is unknown, the African-American baritone Roland Hayes, a friend of Quilter's whom the composer artistically encouraged, performed two of the songs in Paris in 1924 with the composer at the piano. "Cherry Valley" with string parts was recorded by Quilter and baritone Mark Raphael, included in the CD packaged with Valerie Langfield's *Roger Quilter: His Life and Music*, The Boydell Press, 2002.

Five Shakespeare Songs, Op. 23 (Second Set)

Fear no more the heat o' the sun
Under the greenwood tree
It was a lover and his lass
Take, O take those lips away
Hey, ho, the wind and the rain

Three of the songs were composed in 1919. "Fear no more" was composed in 1921. "It was a lover and his lass" was originally composed as a duet in 1919; the solo version was composed in 1921. Unlike the Shakespeare songs of Op. 6, which are conceptually linked, this opus is simply a collection of songs. The first song of the set was dedicated to the memory of Robin Hollway, Quilter's friend from Oxford who died in suicide in 1921. Three of the songs were dedicated to Quilter's close friend Walter Creighton, a singer in his youth and the artist who premiered Ralph Vaughan Williams' *Songs of Travel*. The songs have been often recorded. Among others, Peter Pears recorded "Fear no more;" Janet Baker was among the artists who recorded "It was a lover and his lass." The first, third and fourth songs were recorded by Quilter and baritone Mark Raphael, recordings included on the CD packaged with *Roger Quilter: His Life and Music*, by Valerie Langfield, The Boydell Press, 2002.

Two Songs, Op. 26

In the highlands
Over the land is April

Composed 1922. Published by Elkin, 1922. "Over the land is April" was recorded by Quilter and baritone Mark Raphael, included on the CD packaged with *Roger Quilter: His Life and Music*, by Valerie Langfield, The Boydell Press, 2002.

Old English Popular Songs

Barbara Allen
Drink to Me Only with Thine Eyes
The Jolly Miller
Over the Mountains
Three Poor Mariners

Composed c1917-1921. Published individually by Winthrop Rogers, 1921. Quilter made arrangements for piano trio of "Drink to Me Only" and "Three Poor Mariners," calling the set *Two Old English Tunes* (published by Winthrop Rogers, 1917). In the 1940s Quilter included the five songs first known as *Old English Popular Songs* in *The Arnold Book of Old Songs*, dedicated to Arnold Vivian, the composer's favorite nephew who was killed in World War II. Though individual sheets had been previously released, the assembled collection was first published by Boosey & Hawkes, 1950.

Sources Consulted:

Stephen Banfield, *Sensibility and English Song* (Cambridge University Press, 1985).

Percy Grainger, *The Farthest North of Humanness: Letters of Percy Grainger 1901-1914,* ed. Kay Dreyfus (Melbourne: MMB Music, Inc., 1985).

Percy Grainger, *The All-Round Man: Selected Letters of Percy Grainger 1914-1961,* ed. Malcom Gilles and David Pear (Oxford University Press, 1994).

Trevor Hold: *The Walled-In Garden: A Study of the Songs of Roger Quilter* (London: Thames, 1996).

Salan Keiler, *Marian Anderson: A Singer's Journey* (New York: Simon & Schuster, 2000).

Valerie Langfield, *Roger Quilter: His Life and Music* (Woodbridge, Suffolk: The Boydell Pres, 2002).

The New Grove Dictionary of Music and Musicians, ed. S. Sadie and J. Tyrrell (London: Macmillan, 2001).

Michael Pilkington, *English Solo Song Guides to the Repertoire of Gurney, Ireland, Quilter, Warlock* (London: Duckworth, 1989).

Also in THE VOCAL LIBRARY

POPULAR BALLADS FOR CLASSICAL SINGERS
Concert Arrangements by Richard Walters
00740138 High Voice
00740139 Low Voice

Wonderfully complex, sophisticated and stylish art music arrangements of classic songs by Richard Rodgers, Cole Porter and George Gershwin, designed for a classical singer and pianist. As one performer put it, "The arrangements are so rich they become art songs on their own." **Rodgers songs:** The Sweetest Sounds • I Have Dreamed • You're Nearer. **Porter songs:** I Am in Love • I Concentrate on You • I Hate You Darling. **Gershwin songs:** They Can't Take That Away from Me • A Foggy Day/Love Walked In • Nice Work If You Can Get It • Love Is Here to Stay.

THE CHRISTMAS COLLECTION
Edited by Richard Walters
00740153 High Voice
00740154 Low Voice

A large resource of over 50 songs for holiday services and events, designed for a lifetime of use. Material includes art songs, classic popular songs, and arrangements for solo voice and piano. A few bonus duets are included, and selected songs have solo instrumental obbligatos.

CONTENTS: *Art Songs/Traditional Songs*—A Christmas Carol (Dello Joio) • The Birthday of a King (Neidlinger) • Bright Star (Dello Joio) • Epiphanias (Wolf) • Ermuntre Dich (Bach) • Gesù Bambino (Yon) • Holy Infant's Lullaby • I Stand Here at the Cradleside (duet) (Karg-Elert) • I Wonder as I Wander (Niles) • Jesus of Nazareth (Gounod) • Noël des enfants qui n'ont plus de masions (Debussy) • Nun wandre Maria (Wolf) • O Holy Night (Adam) • O Jesulein süss (Bach) • Schlafendes Jesuskind (Wolf) • A Slumber Song of the Madonna (Head) • The Virgin's Slumber Song (Reger) • *Weihnachtslieder* (Cornelius) • What Songs Were Sung (Niles). *Carol Arrangements, most arr. by Richard Walters*—Angels We Have Heard on High (Les anges dans nos campagnes) (duet) • Bring a Torch, Jeannette, Isabella (Un flambeau, Jeanette, Isabelle) (with violin) • Caroling, Caroling • Deck the Hall (with flute) • The First Noel • Go, Tell It on the Mountain • The Holly and the Ivy (duet, with flute) • I Saw Three Ships • In the Bleak Midwinter • It Came Upon the Midnight Clear • Jesus, Jesus, Rest Your Head • Lo, How a Rose E'er Blooming (with violin) • O Hearken Ye • Once in Royal David's City • Silent Night • Some Children See Him • The Star Carol • This Is Christmas • Wexford Carol. *Classic Popular Christmas Songs*—The Christmas Song (arr. Walters) • The Christmas Waltz • Do You Hear What I Hear • I Heard the Bells on Christmas Day • I'll Be Home for Christmas • The Most Wonderful Time of the Year • Silver Bells • White Christmas (arr. Walters).

Also in THE VOCAL LIBRARY

THE SACRED COLLECTION
Edited by Richard Walters
00740155 High Voice
00740156 Low Voice

A huge collection of 70 sacred songs for classical singers, spanning an enormous range of literature, including art songs, traditional songs, classic Burleigh spiritual arrangements (experts on African-American spirituals contend they are for singers of all ethnic heritages), and distinctive concert arrangements of hymns and folksongs by Richard Walters. There are four duets included. This collection will be as useful in the voice studio as in every working singer's repertoire and every church music library.

CONTENTS: *Sacred Art Songs/Traditional Sacred Songs*—Agnus Dei (Bizet) • Ave Maria (Franck) • Ave Maria (Schubert) • Ave Maria (Bach/Gounod) • Be Near Me Still (Hiller) • Biblical Songs (Dvořák) *complete set* (Clouds and Darkness • Lord, Thou Art My Refuge • Hear My Prayer • God Is My Shepherd • I Will Sing New Songs • Hear My Prayer, O Lord • By the Waters of Babylon • Turn Thee to Me • I Will Lift Up Mine Eyes • Sing Ye a Joyful Song • Bist du bei mir (Stölzel, previously attributed to Bach) • Crucifixus (Faure) • Dank sei Dir, Herr (Ochs, previously attributed to Handel) • Entreat Me Not to Leave Thee (Gounod) • Evening Hymn (Purcell) • Evening Prayer from *Hansel and Gretel* (duet) (Humperdinck) • He That Keepeth Israel (Schlösser) • The Holy City (Weatherly and Adams) • Jesu, Joy of Man's Desiring (Bach) • O Divine Redeemer (Gounod) • The Palms (Fauré) • Panis Angelicus (Franck) • There Is a Green Hill Far Away (Gounod). *Spirituals, Arr. by Harry T. Burleigh*—Balm in Gilead • By an' By • Couldn't Hear Nobody Pray • Deep River • Didn't My Lord Deliver Daniel • Don't You Weep When I'm Gone • Go Down, Moses • Go, Tell It on the Mountain • The Gospel Train • He's Just the Same Today • I Don't Feel No-Ways Tired • I Stood on the River of Jordan • I Want to Be Ready • Let Us Cheer the Weary Traveler • Little David, Play on Your Harp • My Lord, What a Mornin' • My Way's Cloudy • Nodoby Knows the Trouble I've Seen • O Rocks, Don't Fall on Me • Oh, Didn't It Rain • Sinner, Please Don't Let This Harvest Pass • Sometimes I Feel Like a Motherless Child • Steal Away • Swing Low, Sweet Chariot • 'Tis Me, O Lord • Wade in the Water • Weepin' Mary • You May Bury Me in the East. *Concert Arrangements of Hymns & Sacred Folksongs, Arr. by Richard Walters*—Ah, Holy Jesus • All Creatures of Our God and King (duet) • Be Thou My Vision • Come, Thou Fount of Every Blessing • How Can I Keep from Singing (duet) • How Firm a Foundation • Just a Closer Walk with Thee • Let Us Break Bread Together • Now Thank We All Our God • O for a Thousand Tongues to Sing • Praise to the Lord, the Almighty • This Is My Father's World • We Are Climbing Jacob's Ladder (duet) • Wondrous Love (duet).

Also in THE VOCAL LIBRARY

FRANZ SCHUBERT: 100 SONGS
Edited by Steven Stolen & Richard Walters
00740027 High Voice
00740028 Low Voice

A major new edition, newly researched, with new music engravings, historical notes on each song, a poet index and line by line translations for study. Unlike other Schubert editions, the complete cycles *Die Winterreise* and *Die schöne Müllerin* are deliberately not included, since in their entirety they are not useful to most singers. (*Schwanengesang* is included in its entirety, however.) This leaves a great deal of room for a rich selection of individual songs. In the introductory notes for each song you will find information about the song's composition, its biographical context in Schubert's life, early performances, and comments about poets.

CONTENTS: Abendstern • Abschied • Am Grabe Anselmos • Am See (Bruchmann) • Am See (Mayrhofer) • An den Mond (Goethe) • An den Mond (Hölty) • An den Tod • An die Entfernte • An die Geliebte • An die Laute • An die Leier • An die Musik • An die Nachtigall • An die Sonne • An Schwager Kronos • An Silvia • Auf dem Strom (*high voice only*) • Auf dem Wasser zu singen • Auf der Bruck • Das Abendrot (*low voice only*) • Dass sie hier gewesen! • Der Alpenjäger • Der Hirt auf dem Felsen (*high voice only*) • Der Jüngling an der Quelle • Der König in Thule • Der Musensohn • Der Neugierige • Der Tod und das Mädchen • Der Wanderer • Der Zwerg • Die Allmacht • Die böse Farbe • Die Forelle • Die junge Nonne • Die liebe Farbe • Die Liebe hat gelogen • Die Männer sind méchant! • Die Unterscheidung • Du bist die Ruh • Du liebst mich nicht • Ellens Gesang I (Raste Krieger) • Ellens Gesang II (Jäger, ruhe von der Jagd!) • Ellens Gesang III (Ave Maria!) • Erlafsee • Erlkönig • Erster Verlust • Frühlingsglaube • Ganymed • Geheimes • Grenzen der Menschheit • Gretchen am Spinnrade • Gruppe aus dem Tartarus • Heidenröslein • Heliopolis I • Heliopolis II • Herbst • Hoffnung • Im Abendrot • Im Frühling • Im Haine • Im Walde • Jägers Abendlied • Klaglied • Lachen und Weinen • Liebe schwärmt auf allen Wegen • Lied der Mignon (Heiß mich nicht reden) • Lied der Mignon (So lasst mich scheinen) • Lied der Mignon (Nur wer die Sehnsucht kennt) • Litanei • Meeres Stille • Memnon • Mignons Gesang (Kennst du das Land?) • Nacht und Träume • Nachtstück • Nachtviolen • Rastlose Liebe • Romanze (*low voice only*) • Schäfers Klagelied) • *Schwanengesang:* Liebesbotschaft • Kriegers Ahnung • Frühlingssehnsucht • Ständchen (Rellstab) • Aufenthalt • In der Ferne • Abschied (Rellstab) • Der Atlas • Ihr Bild • Das Fischermädchen • Die Stadt • Am Meer • Der Doppelgänger • Die Taubenpost • Sehnsucht • Sei mir gegrüßt • Seligkeit • Ständchen (Shakespeare) • Suleika I • Verklärung • Wandrers Nachtlied I • Wandrers Nachtlied II • Wohin?

FOR MORE INFORMATION, SEE YOUR LOCAL MUSIC DEALER,
OR WRITE TO:

HAL•LEONARD®
CORPORATION
7777 W. BLUEMOUND RD. P.O. BOX 13819 MILWAUKEE, WI 53213

Visit Hal Leonard online at **www.halleonard.com**